PETER THREE EIGHT
THE PILOTS' STORY

XP-38 after it was rolled out of the hangar in January 1939.

PETER THREE EIGHT

THE PILOTS' STORY

JOHN STANAWAY

PICTORIAL HISTORIES PUBLISHING COMPANY
MISSOULA, MONTANA

LIBRARY OF CONGRESS
CATALOG CARD NUMBER 86-60128

ISBN 0-933126-73-5

First Printing: November 1986
Second Printing: February: 1988
Third Printing: February 1991
Fourth Printing: July 1995

About the Author

John Stanaway was born in Minneapolis, Minnesota, on Oct. 23, 1942. He began his enthusiasm for the P-38 when his father brought back a piece of one from the Aleutians after World War II. After hearing all the stories about how wonderful the Lockheed was, he decided to learn as much as he could. Throughout his life, which included a tour with the Air Force in Southeast Asia support during the Vietnam War and degrees with the University of Minnesota and Metropolitan State University in St. Paul, Minnesota, he has maintained a love for aviation and its lore.

Stanaway has written numerous articles for magazines such as Air Pictorial, Military History, Aircraft Illustrated and Fine Scale Modeler. He is the author of *Cobra in the Clouds: a combat history of the 39th Fighter Squadron* and is working on a book about Neel Kearby with the 348th Fighter Group.

PICTORIAL HISTORIES PUBLISHING COMPANY
713 South Third West
Missoula, Montana 59801

Contents

Introduction

*T*HE LOCKHEED P-38 LIGHTNING FIGHTER was one of America's most important contributions to the Allied victory in World War II. It was the first U.S. fighter that seriously challenged the German Messerschmitt 109. It was also the first Allied fighter capable of wresting control of the air from Mitsubishi's vaunted A6m Zero. Well over 3,000 Axis aircraft were credited as shot down by Lightnings; the P-38 became the symbol of ultimate victory over Japan.

One example that illustrates the usefulness of the P-38 is its record in the period from the end of the North African campaign through the Sicily invasion. It is well recorded that the P-38 caused havoc with enemy aerial transport well out into the Mediterranean during the closing days of the fighting in Tunisia and hastened the departure of Axis troops from North Africa. During the Sicilian invasion more than one-third of the approximately 150 American air victories were credited to the three P-38 groups of the Twelfth Air Force, although those three groups constituted only about one-quarter of the American fighter force. Evidence indicates that Adolf Hitler was concerned enough by the Sicilian invasion that he withdrew his forces from an engagement at Kursk. The battle of Kursk was pivotal for the Russians and preceded their inexorable march to Berlin.

It is undeniable that the P-38 was an important factor in the American role in World War II. But what of the men who flew those P-38s? What kind of person did it take to fly one of the most unique fighters of the war into the hotbeds of combat? Were they unrelenting professionals, or were they careless daredevils who braved a maverick trail in the relentless dice game of war?

An answer of sorts may be found in a comparison of the top two American aces, both of whom scored all their victories in the P-38. Dick Bong was as reticent and shy on the ground as he was dynamic in the air. There was an amazing transformation when he stepped into the cockpit of his Lightning. The soft-spoken and smiling kid on the ground became an outrageous maniac in the air. His comrades in other Fifth Air Force fighters over New Guinea were astonished to hear the usually reverent Lutheran towhead from Poplar, Wisconsin, swear like a sailor over the radio when he went into combat.

Bong and his pal, John G. "Jump" O'Neill, were learning to fly the P-38 in Gen. George Kenney's Fourth Air Force around Hamilton Field, California, when they first got into trouble for breaking air discipline. Bong had been buzzing a friend's house and generally sucking up the neighborhood with the wake of his P-38 while "Jump" O'Neill smartly looped the center span of the Golden Gate bridge. (General Kenney loved to impute the Golden Gate looping stunt to Bong, but all written evidence indicates that O'Neill was the only perpetrator of that act.)

Bong and O'Neill were duly slapped on the wrist for their indiscretion, but Kenney was aware that they had the spirit and skill that he wanted in the pilots who would make up the combat command that he would form in New Guinea. Bong became the complete master of the P-38 and never completely lost his abandon in aerial combat. It was only through the tempering effect of someone like Tommy Lynch that Bong's true potential was realized. Lynch was a mathematically precise combat leader and Bong counted him a close personal friend. Somehow, Lynch was able to put an effective rein on Bong's exuberance and helped direct the energies that would propel him to become the leading American ace.

Tom McGuire is a different story. He also was the complete master of the P-38 and appreciated its capabilities. However, the similarities end there. McGuire talked constantly and his voice had the effect of a rasping file on the nerves of his comrades. He was an insecure person who enjoyed needling those with superior prestige. He was also a martinet who let none doubt his authority over a flight or squadron or whatever he happened to command at the moment.

But he was respected for his flying and fighting ability and is also reputed to have been fearless in combat, evinced by his willingness to engage in turns with the redoubtable Zero. Bong and McGuire flew together only briefly but successfully. They also reportedly bunked together at General Kenney's insistence. McGuire is also the only person reported to have broken Bong's cool to the point that his needling persuaded Bong to pack up his gear and move out in a huff.

In short, Bong was universally liked and respected for his gentle nature on the ground and fierce reputation in the air. McGuire was generally disagreeable, but his comrades overlooked his acid nature in view of his tremendous reputation as a P-38 combat leader.

There were other notables who flew the P-38 during World War II. Charles Lindbergh flew the Lightning and was impressed by its technical capability. The French writer Antoine de Saint-Exupery flew photo-reconnaissance Lightnings with his old Armee de L'Air unit and was lost on a flight over southern France. There are others, some famous and some not so famous, who are included briefly in this book. The author has been privileged to meet and know many of them; he dedicates this volume to their character and courage.

Foreword
to the Second Edition

In May of 1987 I had the privilege of attending the 50th anniversary reunion of P-38 pilots in Los Angeles. There was some trepidation, I confess, at the prospect of meeting some of those fellows that I had written about.

There was no need for concern. The one conclusion that I had reached long ago held true; most P-38 veterans are nice people who are slow to anger and appreciate a good joke or story. They greeted me warmly and affirmed my effort in *Peter Three Eight*.

It was warming to get that sort of feedback. One historian even went so far as to tell me that the book was about the best of its kind he had read. I was flushed in embarrassment, but what could I say to such a truthful gentleman!

The reunion also gave me an opportunity to reacquaint myself with the cockpit of the venerable Lightning when we went to Chino for a demonstration of Lefty Gardner's P-38H cum P-38L. I again tried to impress the crowds by deftly running up the ladder, carefully starting out with the left foot on the left side of the cockpit section. I made it up without incident and sat in the cockpit once more (the thing had seemingly shrunk since 1975!). Coming down was another matter when I probed for the ground from the last step and couldn't find land. I thanked the youngster who guided my foot to the concrete with as much dignity as I could muster.

However, aside from the positive memories (I will never forget the sight of Lefty Gardner taxiing his P-38 with its heavily blurping engine across the grass field with dozens of people following it like children behind some giant pied piper about to delight them wtih a magical flying show) there were some complaints with my treatment of the story —some lighthearted and a few not so lighthearted.

One of the first people that I met was Phil Goldstein (Graham) who appears without much further explanation in the 15th Air Force chapter of the first edition. He told me that he and Bob Seidman flew together on Seidman's last mission and that they both wanted to give the Nazi superman a thorough thumb-nosing. While Seidman had a large Solomon Seal or Star of David painted on the nose of his P-38 Goldstein went one step further and painted the·words "Jewboy" on the left side and the same name in German on the right engine of his P-38! Is it any wonder that I like these P-38 guys?

Another 15th Air Force pilot who had a somewhat less-than-serious bone to pick with me was Jack Walker of the 82nd Fighter Group. Somehow I neglected to credit Jack with his four confirmed victories scored between March 1943 and January 1944. It would not have mattered that much to Jack except for the fact that he got one more victory which he could not get confirmed no matter how much he tried. Thus, he had been frustrated since the end of the war by the knowledge possessed only by himself that he was a P-38 ace. The frustration was so acute at one point that when Jack heard that a former Luftwaffe ace was touring the U.S. and Canada by air he tried to get the German's flight plan on the chance that it was not too late to get one more confirmed victory!

Walker laughed at the story when I told it to him at the reunion. Then he asked how long ago the Luftwaffe ace had taken off on the tour.

My old benefactor Colonel Obie Taylor did properly take me to task for allowing the impression to exist that the 14th Fighter Group was *ever* in danger of disgrace. I did use that word too loosely in regard to a misguided message that some ill-informed source saw fit to send out. Let me make three facts very clear: (1) The 14th Fighter Group is one of the outstanding American units of the war—period! (2) The USAAF never intended to retire the 14th in disgrace; the group was simply shot to pieces under the pressure of the hellish operations it was required to undertake and really didn't have the pilots or planes to continue. (3) I included that benighted message primarily to describe how Obie Taylor and the 14th Fighter Group became introduced to each other.

I regret any impression emanating from my pen that the 14th could be less than the great outfit it was. However that may be, I still have to meet anyone who thinks badly of the illustrious 14th and I trust that a malevolence darker than I can conjure would be required to tarnish its bright star.

Acknowledgments

Pilots, writers, aviation historians and various organizations who helped complete this volume include:

Pilots: Tom Maloney, Cecil Quesseth, Jack Ilfrey, Dick Lee, Darrell Welch, Jay Robbins, William Giroux, Dick West, Cornelius Smith, Obie Taylor, Jack Lenox, William Armstrong, Nathaniel Raley, William Leverette, Bill Harris, Rex Barber, Art Heiden, Ralph Englehart, Don Penn, Gerald Brown, W.C. DuBose, John Lowell, Ralph Wandrey, C.W. Gupton, John Tilley, Charles King, Richard Smith, Stanley Andrews, John Lane, William Broadfoot, Bob Hanson, Marion Kirby, Ernest Ambort, George Laven.

Writers and historians: Jeff Ethell, John Lambert, Ernest McDowell, Barbara Johnson Curtis, Paul McDaniel, Charles Mayer, Mike Gregg, Ken Ring.

Organizations: 367th Fighter Group Association, National Records Center, Simpson Historical Center.

To each of these I give much credit and many thanks. And finally, thanks to my wife, Susan, who gave cheerfully and freely to the cause.

Front view of the YP-38.

AAHS

Chapter 1
About the Lightning...

*O*N THE CLEAR, STAR-FILLED NIGHT OF December 31, 1938, the P-38 Lightning fighter began its journey to operational life with all the intrigue of the era in which it was conceived. Strange canvas-covered forms on the beds of several trucks were attended by a police and military escort in a convoy from the Lockheed Burbank factory to the Army hangars at March Field. There was, however, little surreptitious purpose in the night move. In spite of the understandable need for extreme security measures, the late-night move was actually timed to observe Lockheed's highway permit, which expired at midnight. After arriving at the field, the P-38 components remained in a tightly guarded hangar for about two weeks.

Notwithstanding a mishap in which the XP-38 ended in a ditch after brake failure, the Lightning's first flight took place on January 27, 1939. Lt. Ben Kelsey was familiar with the fighter already, but studied it carefully before he made the final ground runs and sent the graceful fighter along the runway on its first takeoff. In the next few seconds indications of the P-38's future problems became evident. The Lightning bucked and shook wildly under Kelsey's hand. With a great deal of skill and effort Kelsey managed to steady the big fighter and flew it for half an hour before gingerly making a landing. It was discovered that a wing flap had failed and made control extremely difficult. This was only one indication of many that would lead to a reputation for the P-38 for high performance and dangerous flight characteristics.

The Lockheed Lightning would pioneer, among other things, experience with the phantom force known as compressibility. When the P-38 was dived to the maximum of its design limit, the air surrounding the fuselage would become an obstruction because it couldn't be guided into the slipstream quickly enough to prevent interference with the aircraft's performance. Later, the P-38 was the source of much

P-38J-5 and F5B-1 modified from the J-5. Delivery completed by October 1943.   AAHS

-1-

of the research used in the streamlining of jet aircraft after the war. As it was, a fear of the P-38 grew in the minds of some pilots. The problem persisted to some degree until the sub-series reached the J-25 and L models, which incorporated dive control flaps that countered the compressibility syndrome.

In general, the P-38 program lagged because of manufacturing problems as well as the unfamiliar physical forces to which the Lockheed was subjected. It wasn't until September 1940 that the first YP-38s were produced for Army evaluation and first production P-38s began to appear in August 1941. Another negative facet was attributed to the Lightning after the aircraft was involved in a number of accidents stemming from flat belly spins. It became forbidden for pilots to turn into an engine with reduced power since there was a strong feeling that the aircraft would go into a spin under such conditions. Subsequent combat experience would dispel such fear, but until the P-38 was tried in hard battle situations, the myths would haunt the minds of many pilots and color their attitude in operational service.

Another delay in the P-38 program came from a Congressional investigation, which would be one of two government trials the Lightning would undergo before the end of World War II. The fact that the P-38 was the first fighter plane in squadron service to utilize the turbo-supercharger and that it was of unconventional design anyway must have elicited many technical problems that drew attention from official sources. An unfortunate incident may have also further diminished the image of the P-38 when veteran test pilot Ralph Virden was killed in the crash of a YP-36 in November 1941.

But the deployment of the P-38 would be carried on, and, by the time of the Pearl Harbor attack, about sixty-five Lightnings would be counted on inventory. By early spring of 1942 the 1st, 14th and 55th fighter groups would be in various stages of training with the Lockheed fighter. The reputation of the P-38 grew into that of one of the hottest and most dangerous fighter aircraft in the sky. Only through the experience of brave and eager combat pilots would the true nature of the P-38 emerge, the nature of an aircraft that would rank as one of the finest warplanes that ever flew.

Conceived from a requirement for a high-altitude interceptor, the P-38 would be called upon to fill a number of combat roles with varying degrees of success. The most frequent use mentioned within these pages will be that of escort fighter. It should be remembered that the P-38 was a twin-engined aircraft competing with single-engined fighters and that very few twin-engined fighters achieved the record of the Lightning. Apart from the Junkers 88 and De Havilland Mosquito, no other reciprocating twin-engined fighter comes close to challenging the Lockheed Lightning in total performance record. The proof is in the telling.

YP-38 being rolled out of bldg. 214.

AAHS

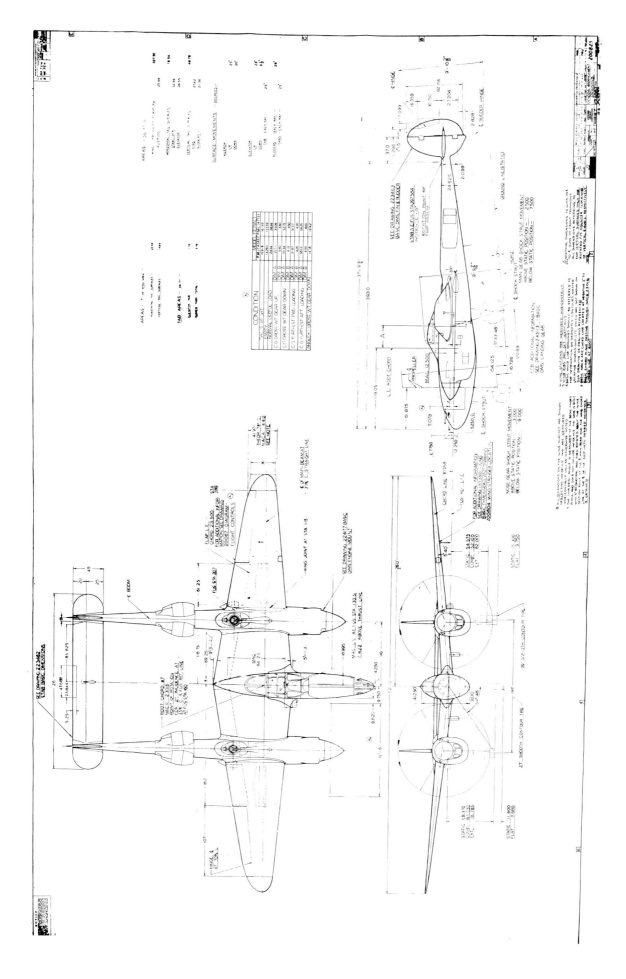

Basic layout of the P-38L.
Lockheed

-3-

P-38L banks to port. L model is easily identified from this angle by the installation of the wing light. Retractable light under port wing was standard on all previous marks.   Lockheed

P-38J-20 ex-AAF machine photographed after the war.
via Ken Ring

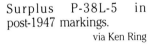

Surplus P-38L-5 in post-1947 markings.
via Ken Ring

Chapter 2
Into Battle

*H*OW MUCH OF THE STORY IS TRUE CANnot be determined for certain because most of the sources trace back to wartime Lockheed press releases. But what is certain is that the ringing whine of the Lightning's Allison engines was probably heard by the Japanese for the first time over the Coral Sea in May 1942. It was then that Capt. Karl Polifka reportedly flew his reconnaissance F-4 Lightning over the Japanese fleet, which was staging for the upcoming great battle, and gave the enemy a rude preview of what to expect from the American fighter.

Captain Polifka had been running what had been termed "a one man show" over New Guinea with F-4s of the 8th Photographic Squadron. Actually, the 8th Squadron was no more than a single flight of four Lightnings, which arrived in Australia on April 7. No effective photographic missions were flown before three of the Lightnings were rendered inoperable by accidents or technical malfunctions. Only Polifka in his F-4, named "Faintin' Floozie," continued into operational status. It was an inauspicious beginning for a unit that would render such distinguished photo-recon service in the Southwest Pacific.

Whatever the circumstances, Polifka was able to point his F-4 over the Japanese ships on that day in May while they plied the azure water of the Coral Sea. Dutifully occupied with recording the details of Japanese naval strength, Captain Polifka disregarded the almost certain presence of Japanese fighter cover. The first indication Polifka had that Japanese fighters were in the area was the alarming pattern of bullet holes that suddenly appeared in his Lightning's wings. Looking around, he saw the black cowls and gray wings of Zero fighters bearing down for the kill. Trembling from the shock, his hand set both throttles full to the stops and the F-4 gave the Japanese their surprise for the morning when it suddenly left them behind in the distance.

Polifka's problems were not ended, however, for a Zero's cannon shell had disabled one of his engines and he was forced to feather the propeller for fear of an explosion. Seriously crippled in this way, the F-4 should have been easy meat for the Japanese fighters that were desperately trying to close the gap. Again, wartime reports make much of the story open to suspicion, but Polifka reportedly outflew his pursuers to the point where he got above one of them

Warrant Officer Schrader, Roland Baker and Fred Hargesheimer by Polifka's "Fainting Floozie II." August 1942.   Norbert Krane

Capt. Karl Polifka studies photographic mosaic.

Colonel Polifika during a subsequent tour in Italy.   USAF

and forced the Zero down into a water landing.

Whatever the specific details may have been, the big, tough Lightning and Karl Polifka's skill brought plane and pilot back to New Guinea with valuable photo intelligence. The Japanese had received their first look at the aircraft that would give them no small amount of trouble and Karl Polifka had begun his career as one of the Army's premier photo-reconnaissance pilots.

Subsequent to the Battle of the Coral Sea, Japanese forces invaded the Aleutian Islands; the P-38 had its second chance at combat in as many months during the defense of American territory proper. Because of the imminent Japanese threat in the Aleutians, the 28th Bomb Group was reinforced with a P-38 squadron early in June 1942. Some records indicate that three H6K "Mavis" flying boats were destroyed at anchor just off Kiska by P-38s in their first sorties late in June.

The first confirmed P-38 victory of the war came on August 4 when a flight of P-38s was vectored through typical nasty North Pacific weather to intercept three Mavis flying boats that were apparently on patrol for the American PBY tenders. The Lightnings found the Japanese and roared through the formation to down a pair of the aircraft while the third managed to escape into cloud. Effective Japanese bomber patrols ended with this final loss of four-engine Mavis seaplanes.

Another unit, the 343rd Fighter Group, was formed in September and assigned to the Aleutian front. One of the pilots who came out with the 343rd's 54th Fighter Squadron and its Lightnings was Capt. George Laven, who had been stationed in the Alaskan theater for some months and would claim some unique records with the P-38. On September 3, during an attack on enemy shipping in Kiska Harbor, Laven and Lt. Walton strafed and damaged installations and moored ships within the harbor. Probably in the same general area that day Laven caught and downed a Japanese fighter he found in the air. In little more than a week, another Japanese fighter fell to the guns of Laven's P-38 as he continued to establish his remarkable record.

Sometime late in November 1942, Captain Laven was ordered to deliver his P-38, which had received some battle damage, to a modification center in Alaska. The captain was disgusted to find that no center in the theater of operations was in service. With determination, Laven pointed his Lockheed toward a repair depot that he knew was operating—near his home in San Antonio, Texas! With the tail damage of his airplane finally repaired, and after a pleasant brief reunion with his family and friends, Captain Laven simply took his aircraft back to the Aleutians and continued with his war.

Laven's "Itsy Bitsy" in San Antonio.　　　George Laven

George Laven with his mother and brother in San Antonio.　　　Laven

Laven in Adak about April 1943.　　　Laven

There seemed to be an abundance of accessory dangers in the Aleutian campaign. The weather was the most adverse in the world and more planes were probably lost to the elements than to enemy action. One lucky P-38 pilot survived what should have been a fatal accident. While his aircraft was running at high speed on steel plank runway that was partially covered with water, the P-38 suddenly swerved and landed upside down in a water-filled ditch. The shaken pilot managed to open his side window and crawl out, parachute and all, to safety. When the Lightning was finally dredged from the water, measurements taken of the window-panel opening seemed to indicate that the escape was impossible.

Another less fortunate accident occurred on September 14, 1942, when B-24s were escorted by P-38s and brand new P-39s on a mission to Kiska. Major Jackson and Lieutenant Crowe were lost as their P-38s collided while they were chasing the same Japanese fighter. The P-38 would develop an apparent propensity for collision during the war, perhaps because the engine cowlings partially blocked pilot

vision from the quarter. The P-38E, which initially equipped the units in the Aleutian campaign, may have also been unsuitable for existing weather conditions, for that particular model of the Lightning was placed on the restricted list late in 1942. As it was, many pilots were lost to the elements. Out of thirty-three pilots in George Laven's original squadron, only ten survived to the end of their tour.

George Laven did survive to finish off his record for the Aleutian tour. On February 13, 1943, he claimed two more Zeros to make him one of the high-scoring fighter pilots in the theater. But his scoring was not yet quite complete. He would return from the Aleutians and eventually be assigned to the 49th Fighter Group when that unit was based in the Philippines. He would find old comrades from his sub-zero war such as Tom McGuire, Jerry Johnson and Wallace Jordan. And he would claim one last but distinctive victory.

Perhaps one combat has some relevance to the P-38s initiation into battle. In August 1942, the 1st Fighter Group was staging out of Iceland for its eventual assignment to the Eighth Air Force. The 1st would finally be deployed to the sands of North Africa, far removed from the cold and wet North Atlantic area. But on August 14 the first Army Air Force victory over the Luftwaffe would be won, at least in part, by a Lightning over the rolling Atlantic.

A P-39 flown by Lt. Joseph Shaffer was the first to encounter the four-engine FW200 on the morning of August 14. Shaffer roared onto the tail of the big Luftwaffe raider and fired round after round until he saw flame and smoke slip back from one of the bomber's engines. Lt. Elza K. Shahan was patrolling at a higher level when he noticed the stricken German trying to escape Shaffer's guns. Shahan sent his Lightning into a dive after the fleeing Focke Wulf and put a long burst of fire into the bomber's fuselage. Shahan was so close to the resulting explosion that he was blinded momentarily by the flash. Shahan would go on to North Africa to score at least one more aerial victory but he had made a record for himself and the Lockheed he flew on that gray morning over the Atlantic.

Laven by his P-38 in April 1943.   Laven

Laven with fellow officer in September 1943.   Laven

Laven's P-38 with victory markings in April 1943.   Laven

Lieutenant Archer lost his life in this P-38 on Adak in 1942.   Laven

Chapter 3

Fifth Air Force
from Buna to Rabaul

39th and 9th Fighter Squadrons
as starters

A flip of the coin was all it took for the V Fighter Command's 39th Fighter Squadron to be the first unit in the New Guinea area equipped with P-38 fighters. The choice was fortunate because the 39th's record with the P-38 would sparkle as it had with the P-39.

Several Japanese aircraft had fallen to the eager Airacobra pilots without loss of a single 39th pilot in combat. Some of the 39th pilots who would play prominent roles in the operational success of the P-38 were already doing well against the threat of Japanese warplanes. During the 39th's first tour between May and August 1942, Tom Lynch had accounted for three Zeros and Curran "Jack" Jones shot down a seasoned Japanese ace who was attacking a flight of B-26s over Cape Ward Hunt on June 9.

P-38s began arriving in Australia about the end of summer but problems delayed the 39th's entry into combat. The airplanes themselves were full of faults like leaking intercoolers and improperly sealed fuel cells. Maintenance was also a problem since most mechanics in the area were unfamiliar with the P-38. Thirty-ninth Fighter Squadron ace Lt. Stanley Andrews had come to New Guinea with the P-38s and was dismayed to find that his aircraft had been assembled with the ailerons on the wrong wings!

But the 39th pilots persevered and flew a mix of training and operational patrol flights throughout the end of October and into November. In late November Capt. Bob Faurot dropped a bomb over the Lae runway and downed a Japanese fighter that was taking off and flew straight into the stone-hard curtain of water raised by the explosion. By the beginning of December, Japanese reports indicated sightings of the distinctive two-tailed Lightning; one report for December 26, 1942, by the Japanese Army Air Force's 11th Sentai even recorded an aerial victory over P-38s. (The first V Fighter Command P-38 loss came on January 8, 1943, when a 39th Lightning was missing from a raid on Lae.)

Japanese fighters faced P-38s over New Guinea in earnest on December 27, 1942. Twelve 39th P-38s were scrambled from 14-Mile Drome at Port Moresby at about 11:30 a.m. to intercept a formation of more than twenty-five Japanese fighters and dive-bombers attacking Buna Mission. At about 12:10 the 39th formation arrived over Buna and sighted the enemy dead ahead and slightly to the right.

Capt. Tommy Lynch took his flight of four P-38s into a formation of 11th Sentai Oscars (Nakajima ki-43 fighters) and managed to explode one with his first shot and riddled another so badly that it appeared to be broken in two. This Oscar managed to fly in its heavily damaged condition back to the north coast of New Britain where its pilot crash-landed and was picked up the next day by a Japanese flying boat.

Two other pilots from Lynch's flight fired at the Oscars without success but then attacked the dive-bombers with better results. Dick Bong, a P-38 pilot on loan from the 9th Fighter Squadron, shot at a Val (D3y), which exploded and crashed. Bong then took a short burst at a passing Zero. This aircraft must have been observed crashing by another 39th pilot since it was awarded to Bong as destroyed.

Ken Sparks fired at another Zero, which crashed in the ocean, but then Sparks himself was beset by Zeros and escaped only after his engine was practically shot out of its mounting. While he was trying to make an emergency landing at Dobodura strip number 4, Sparks found a Val crossing his line of flight and delayed his landing long enough to send the Val down smoking with pieces flying off in various directions. When Sparks did finally land, the nosewheel of his P-38 collapsed and he ended up in the dirt.

Meanwhile, the other flights of P-38s were lacing into the Japanese formations. Hoyt Eason claimed two other Zeros and Stanley Andrews shot the fin and rudder off another Zero, which then spun into the Huon Gulf. Charles Gallup was startled when a Zero roared over his P-38 and got out front to present a perfect target. Gallup turned around to clear his tail and was startled again to find more Japanese fighters close behind. Gallup took the time to dispatch the Zero ahead then turned violently to evade his pursuers. With speed borne of terror he eluded the deadly cannon fire.

When the tally was finally counted the exuberant pilots claimed no fewer than twelve Japanese aircraft, but somewhat cooler heads prevailed and eleven Japanese were officially credited. Japanese records, however, list only two fighters lost and two crash-landed and make no mention of the dive-bombers lost. It seems that the best the 39th could claim is six Japanese aircraft lost, including the dive-

Ken Sparks' #33 after it was damaged on Dec. 31, 1942.

Krane

bombers. Nevertheless, it was a landmark victory for the young P-38 pilots—Sparks' P-38 was the only one to suffer major damage that day.

On the last day of 1942, the 39th met the enemy again and set the pattern for future operations with P-38s. Twelve Zeros attempted to oppose a formation of bombers heading for Lae on December 31, 1942. They failed to reckon, however, with eleven P-38s of the 39th Fighter Squadron. Tom Lynch led the 39th down into a head-on pass and exploded the lead Zero. Ken Sparks claimed yet another pair of Japanese aircraft but his P-38 was damaged again when he collided with one of his victories and came home minus a wingtip. Dick Bong had a frustrating day when he fired at no fewer than six enemy planes and managed to claim only one probable. It was not an impressive performance for the pilot who would become the leading American ace of all time!

The star of the day was Hoyt Eason. He managed to get on the tails of three Zeros and send them all crashing into the jungles around Lae airstrip. Again, no P-38s were lost and Sparks once more flew the only American fighter to receive serious damage.

Japanese records make no mention at all of losses on this date but there can be no doubt that the P-38s were making the enemy painfully aware of their presence. With the nine Zeros claimed on December 31, the P-38s of the Fifth Air Force had claimed at least a dozen victories for no permanent losses. In addition, with the victory of December 31, the first P-38 ace of the Southwest Pacific was created when Hoyt Eason was given credit for his fifth air victory.

During this period the Allies went decidedly on the offensive. With the Buna area secured, heavy pressure was placed on Lae and Salamaua. Raids escorted by P-38s were now possible on these bases and on the convoys that supplied them. Sometimes, to their chagrin, the pilots of the 39th were even pressed into service as dive-bombers.

The next bout of aerial engagements for the P-38s of the 39th came during early January. On January 6, nine Oscars were claimed including two for "Jack" Jones' first P-38 victories. The next day seven more Oscars fell to the 39th out of twenty claimed around Lae by the V Fighter Command.

The 39th was in action over Lae again on January 8 and set a record for Japanese aircraft destroyed in a single day by V Fighter Command squadrons. In three separate escorts the 39th accounted for sixteen Oscars. During the last flight Richard Suehr accounted for two Japanese fighters but a persistent Oscar had the courage to face his P-38 in a head-on duel. Suehr witnessed the Japanese fighter explode during one pass when Dick Bong fired at the Oscar from overhead. The plane fell 18,000 feet into the Huon Gulf for

Curran Jones by his P-38 sometime early in 1943.

Jones

Bong's fifth victory.

After the battles of January, Dick Bong was returned to the 9th Fighter Squadron since that unit was also converting to the P-38. Air activity over Lae was limited due partly to the fact that Japanese forces were obliged to consolidate and renew their attempts to reinforce Lae. Allied forces were victorious in general and the Japanese were defeated in land battles for the first time in New Guinea.

One supreme attempt to reinforce Lae came at the end of February when a Japanese convoy of fourteen destroyers and transports sailed from Rabaul. The convoy was discovered and during the first days of March all eight transports were sunk by Allied bombers in the action that became known as "The Battle of the Bismarck Sea."

Charles King of the 39th Squadron claimed his first Oscar during the battle near Arawe on March 2 and described events of the day in a personal diary:

> With 16 P-38s we escorted 24 B-17s to hit convoy (14 ships) north of New Britain. Bad weather and two flights of us caught three Oscars back of the 17s. Lynch and his wingman after one. He turned back into Jones' flight and Marlett got him. The one my wingman (Randall) went after dove away. But then he pulled up. I got a long shot down then closed up going up. He made only easy rolling turns and turned only when I got close. As I went by Randall also got a shot.
>
> I turned and saw him going straight down, smoking badly. The third ship got away. Weather bad. We returned. The B-17s hit at least three ships sinking at least one.

March 3 proved to be the decisive day when raids by Allied B-17s, B-25s, A-20s and Bristol Beaufighters virtually annihilated the Japanese force. Of 6,000 Japanese troops on the transports fewer than 1,000 survived the battle. Sixteen Japanese fighters that tried to defend the ships fell victim to the P-38s of the 9th and 39th squadrons.

Capt. Charles W. King scored his first victory for the 39th on March 2, 1943, over the Bismarck Sea. He went on to command the 39th when Tom Lynch left for the U.S.

King

Dick Bong was in the 9th Squadron flight covering bombers when seven Oscars appeared below. Bong managed to get in behind one fighter and started it smoking with just one burst. He watched the Oscar fall until it crashed into the water below.

A lion's share of the action fell to the 39th Squadron, which ran straight into a mixed formation of Japanese single-engine fighters. Thirty-Ninth commander Maj. George Prentice led a flight into the heart of the enemy formation and engaged in a snarling dogfight for more than half an hour. In this fight, Paul Stanch scored the first of his eventual ten victories and told the tale later:

> We met 30 Zeros at 18,000 feet and because my motors were acting up and I knew I could climb no higher, I attacked. I saw Prentice fighting a Zero while another crept around behind him. I attacked this and got in a fine short burst when he turned in front of me, followed him down to 8,000 and watched him splash into the sea. I saw three of our bombers attacking and four other ships beyond them, which turned out to be Zeros. The Zero was shadowed by our bombers and failed to see me on his tail. I gave him a two-second burst and he burst into flames.

Richard Smith of the 39th Squadron claimed his second victory when he drew to within 100 yards of an Oscar and fired a burst directly into the cockpit. Stanley Andrews and John "Shady" Lane also caught Japanese fighters attacking the B-17s and sent an Oscar each crashing into the sea.

But this particular victory was not without its heavy toll. Bob Faurot, who had scored the unique bomb victory the previous autumn, led Hoyt Eason and Fred Schifflet down to rescue a Fortress being attacked by numerous enemy fighters. Although he was rated highly as a combat leader, Faurot was simply too worn to put on a fine edge in battle. Although one P-38 was observed flying into cloud and a parachute was seen to descend in the area and Hoyt Eason was identified as ditching his P-38 and entering a life raft, all three P-38s and the B-17 they tried to protect were lost. It was the only multiple loss the 39th would suffer while it flew the P-38, and it was made even more bitter when none of the aircrew ever returned.

The next day continued the grisly business of mopping up the remnants of an already defeated enemy. Several other Japanese fighters persisted in trying to protect the convoy in its death throes and paid a price. Ken Sparks downed two Japanese to tally his ninth victory and Paul Stanch claimed his third victory, an Oscar.

Harry Brown had his first victory over Pearl Harbor during the attack in December 1941 and scored again on March 4, 1943, when he claimed an Oscar with the 9th Squadron. Another pilot who would become an ace with the 9th was wild-flying John O'Neill who literally overwhelmed an A6m-3 version of the Zero, code-named Hamp by the Allies, for his first victory. Consequently, the Battle of the Bismarck Sea came to a merciful close.

Capt. John G. "Jump" O'Neill in the cockpit of his airplane.

O'Neill's P-38 in the autumn of 1943 with eight victory marks. (P-38G-10-Lo 43-2204 "Beautiful Lass")

Eight more Japanese aircraft fell to 9th Fighter Squadron P-38s a few days later over the Bismarck Sea. The 9th was scrambled to meet a raiding force of Mitsubishi G4m Betty bombers covered by Zeros. P-38s and Japanese engaged just after 11:30 a.m. and Jack Mankin downed a Zero for his first victory in the Lightning.

Dick Bong also downed two Zeros in what must have been one of his most harrowing missions. According to his mission report for the day:

Took off just ahead of bombs and climbed up to 24,000 feet. Intercepted the bombers on their way home. Made a 20 degree pass from ahead and above and put a good burst in last bomber. No observed results. 9 Zeros dove on me and I had to dive to 475 mph indicated to get away. Tried to go back for another pass at the bombers but was intercepted by Zeros and chased down to water level. We were headed toward Gasmata. Flew straight until I could only see one Zero behind me.

Made a 180 degree turn and put a long burst into the Zero head on. Instead of only one Zero, there were 9 or more and I turned 5 degrees left and put a short burst into another Zero head on. Both of these (Japanese fighters) had their belly tanks on. Turned 10 degrees right and put a long burst into another Zero from 20 degrees deflection then turned 20 degrees left to observe the results. First two Zeros were burning all around the cockpit and the third was trailing a long column of smoke.

Three Zeros split "s'd" down on me and shot up my left engine and wing while I was running for home. Feathered left engine and landed at home field safely. Claim two certains and one probable.

Bong had been one of the most irrepressible hellions in the skies over New Guinea. Although he was shy and rather quiet on the ground there was an amazing transition when he flung his P-38 around the Pacific sky. He and Ken Sparks had been something like the problem children in the first days of 39th Squadron operations with the P-38.

L to R: Thomas Fowler, Sidney Woods, Jack Mankin and Dick Bong. Woods claimed a Betty, Mankin a Zero and Bong was credited with two Zeros on March 11, 1943. Bong unwittingly turned into a formation of at least nine Zeros and shot two of the fighters down, damaging a third before he got his bullet-riddled P-38 out of harm's way. U.S. Army

Lt. Charles Gallup of the 39th F.S. He scored his first victory during the initial combat of the P-38 with V Fighter Command on Dec. 27, 1942. His last victory came during the Japanese raid on Port Moresby, April 12, 1943, when he downed another Zero.
Carl Bong

But, unlike Sparks who went home rather than submit to strict air discipline, Bong learned valuable lessons like those of the mission of March 11. His natural ability as a fighter pilot became tempered during combat and he matured into a deadly warrior. He was also helped by people like Tommy Lynch who were able to apply effective restraints on Bong's natural exuberance and direct his talent toward highly useful ends. Sparks was also a highly talented pilot credited with at least eleven Japanese warplanes. His career ended tragically when he put a P-38 into a terminal-velocity dive off the coast of California during March 1944 and failed to recover.

John "Shady" Lane sometime in the summer of 1943.
Bong

Paul Stanch who came to the aid of his squadron C.O. during the Bismarck Sea battle and gathered ten victories by the autumn of 1943. King

Wallace Jordan (center) and Grover Fanning (right). Fanning scored the 49th Fighter Group's 200th victory when he downed three Japanese on April 12, 1943, during his first combat.

L to R: *Bottom*—Charles Sullivan, Tom Lynch, Ken Sparks. *Top*—Richard Suehr, John Lane, Stanley Andrews. Photo taken probably late May 1943.

Lynch's first P-38 after he took command of the 39th Sq.

Jim Bong

Opposite: Battle damage on Bong's P-38, March 11, 1943.

Lane

Enter the 80th...

Gen. George Kenney was finally receiving enough P-38s not only to support existing units but to equip a third squadron. Throughout March the 80th Fighter Squadron received enough P-38s to train and work up for operations. The pilots of the 80th were especially keen to get the P-38 into combat and they worked hard to become ready by the end of March.

First victory was enjoyed by the squadron on April 11, 1943. On that day three Val dive-bombers and a Zero fell to the P-38s of the 80th for no losses. Two of the Vals were claimed by Danny Roberts, a talented fighter pilot and legendary leader who managed to claim two Japanese fighters on an earlier mission in the P-39 Airacobra. Roberts would be one of the pilots later selected to form the 475th Fighter Group, the first all-P-38 unit in New Guinea and General Kenney's personal project to create an instant crack outfit.

The next day, Japanese Zeros and Betty bombers once again came over the Owen Stanley Mountains to strike Port Moresby. The V Fighter Command responded frantically and Japanese records indicate that about twenty of their aircraft failed to return. Grover Fanning of the 9th Squadron downed two Bettys and a Zero in his first combat. Charles Gallup and Richard Smith claimed Bettys for the 39th Squadron and Don McGee got another Betty for the 80th's only score for the day.

One big scrap demonstrated the 80th's growing prowess when the squadron escorted transports to the Wau area on May 21. Eleven P-38s were flying at 23,000 feet when a mixed force of Zeros, Hamps and Oscars was sighted in the broken clouds above. The transports were sent back to base while the 80th turned to face the Japanese attack.

John Jones was flying on squadron commander Ed Cragg's wing and dropped his external tanks while the flight turned into the attack. He was unhappy to find that one of the tanks did not release and was even unhappier when tracers appeared passing his cockpit. Jones tried a pushover then changed his mind and rolled over into a dive, indicating 400 mph. Yet the enemy fighters continued to follow the P-38 until he managed to find some welcome clouds. When he emerged from the clouds Jones found a Hamp conveniently below and fired at the Japanese until it burned.

Meanwhile, Cragg had fired at another Hamp and shot off the right wing. Cragg's combat report continues at the point where he and Jones became separated:

> I then went out and came back in to make another attack. A Hamp type aircraft with square wingtips and black and white checkered wing markings made a pass on me from slightly above and at one o'clock. He fired at me and his bullets entered my nose and wings. He passed to within 20 feet in front of me and I saw my bullets enter his cockpit. A slight trail of smoke came from his airplane after I hit him. I looked around and there was a Zero attacking from my rear. My left engine lost manifold pressure and did not have any power. I dove in the direction of Wau in order to get away from him. He finally chandelled away from me and in the meantime I feathered my engine and headed for home.

Final score for the 80th was six fighters definitely shot down for no losses. However, the record of the squadron was only beginning. Exactly one month later, on June 21, 1943, fourteen P-38s of the 80th encountered another formation of Zeros and Oscars in the Lae. Cornelius "Corky" Smith and Bob Adams joined forces to flail into the Japanese

"Corky" Smith standing by his P-38 "Corky Jr." sometime in mid-1943.

ranks and Smith made a remarkable debut in combat by downing three Zeros and probably another, which flew into cloud with numerous bullets and shells in the cockpit. Adams was frustrated by the fact that his guns were jammed but managed to feint attacks, anyway.

George Welch was in the same battle and was also frustrated when his engine cut out while he was following an intended victory down over Salamaua. He managed to correct the P-38 engine and found five other Zeros over Lae. This time he was able to make sure of one Zero, which crashed in flame and smoke, and another, which was literally blown to pieces. Like Brown of the 9th Squadron, Welch had scored victories over Pearl Harbor during the Japanese attack. Just one year afterward Welch downed another three Japanese with his P-39 and on June 21 scored his first victories in the P-38 and his ninth total. The 80th had a total of thirteen victories on June 21 and once again suffered no casualties.

It may seem from the preceding air combats that life was generally easy for the pilots who flew the P-38s. But the losses did mount even if specific casualty figures do not reflect the fact of attrition. For example, two veteran pilots of the 9th Fighter Squadron ended their combat days in March and April of 1943. Lt. Robert Vaught had five confirmed victories including several in the P-38 when he attacked a formation of Japanese fighters on March 29. The next that was heard of Vaught he was badly injured in a crash landing at Wau. William Sells fared even worse during the air battle of April 12 when his P-38 was badly damaged and he crashed to his death while trying to land.

Another pilot who paid a heavy price in the New Guinea air war was 80th Squadron pilot Robert Adams, the brave pilot who had covered "Corky" Smith on the June 21 mission in spite of inoperative guns. Adams had claimed an Oscar on the May 21 mission and totaled his fifth with victories over another Oscar and a twin-engine fighter on August 29. Less than a week later Adams was missing in action when he failed to return from a mission to Wewak on September 2.

Bob Adams, John Jones and Jess Gidley by the officer's club in the 80th F.S. area, July 1943.   USAF

Pilots of the 80th Squadron were also busy on the 21 of July and accounted for eleven Japanese aircraft around Bogadjim. Jay T. Robbins began his scoring tally in a big way by claiming three Zeros. In that summer sky over New Guinea, the big, quiet Texas Aggie began a remarkable career as a P-38 pilot.

Two days later all the P-38 units then active in New Guinea were over the Lae-Salamaua-Bogadjim area at about 10 a.m. Ed Cragg claimed an Oscar and one of the new ki-61 Tony fighters to tally his fifth victory. John Jones also downed two Oscars to become another ace of the 80th Fighter Squadron.

One pilot who scored his first victory and nearly had himself done in was Ralph Wandrey of the 9th Squadron. Wandrey got behind a formation of Oscars over the water off Salamaua and neatly dispatched the trailing plane with some well-aimed bursts. The P-38 pilot was surprised at how easy the whole process was and prepared to take the next Oscar in line. When he turned around to clear his tail, however, Wandrey nearly choked on his heart when he saw the spinners of four Zeros coming down to neatly dispatch him.

Wandrey practically stood the Lightning on its nose and counted three Zeros shooting by his fighter. But where was the fourth? Wandrey snapped his head around and saw the last Zero practically on the verge of a stall, trying to bring its guns to bear. The shaken P-38 pilot set his fighter into a steep climb at 140 mph indicated airspeed and hunched behind the armor plate. Although several cannon shells exploded around the cockpit, the P-38 was able to outclimb the Mitsubishi fighter, which fell away when it shuddered on the stall. Wandrey developed a fondness for the P-38 that day.

July 26 was another day of stellar performance by P-38s of the 9th Fighter Squadron. Nine Lightnings of the 9th engaged an estimated thirty Oscars and Tonys at about 16,000 feet over Salamaua. Eight of the ten Japanese claimed that day fell to the guns of Dick Bong and Jim "Duckbutt" Watkins. Bong claimed two Oscars and two Tonys for his best scoring day of the war. Watkins had to do some convincing of skeptical victory board members but was finally credited with four Tonys.

The other pilot to score on this mission was becoming known in the 9th Squadron as "Johnny Eager" because he insisted on taking every mission that came along and could always be found in the middle of the biggest fights. Gerald Johnson downed his first victories, a Tony and an Oscar, on this mission. He and Watkins became inseparable friends after this mission when each pilot drove a Japanese fighter off the other man's tail.

Two days later the same crew was up on a B-25 escort over New Britain and Watkins was the star again when he shot down three more Oscars. Bong accounted for another

Capt. Gerald Johnson probably sometime in June or July, 1943. The scoreboard on his P-38 shows Johnson's anticipation.

Johnson's #83 with battle damage from July 26, 1943, mission.

P-38G-10 s/n 42-12882 "Charlcie Jeanne." "Duckbutt" Watkins and his ground crew after his spectacular victories of July 1943. Watkins

Oscar and at one point he and "Johnny Eager" Johnson were chasing an Oscar right through the B-25 formation. The two P-38 pilots were so intent on bagging the Japanese fighter that they cried over the radio for the gunners to hold their fire until one of the P-38s could claim the Oscar!

One other mission the 9th flew to the Lae-Saldor area helped to emphasize the growing legend of Jerry Johnson. About one dozen Oscars rose to meet the sixteen P-38s of the 9th on August 2 and bravely fought until all but one Japanese fighter had been shot down. That single Oscar, however, put up a remarkable fight, playing just off the water near the Saldor coast. Every pass made by the P-38 pilots was met with courage and skill and the American fighters finally had to give up the fight because of fuel shortage. That is, they all gave up except for the P-38 of Jerry Johnson. He made just one more pass by the enemy aircraft—to rock his wings in salute. The Japanese returned the gesture and each man turned for home.

...And finally the 475th

General Kenney had finally prevailed on Washington and was promised enough P-38s to equip a new entire group—if he could man it from his own resources. The 11th Air Replacement Depot was scoured for promising material and the existing V Fighter Command squadrons were told early in the spring of 1943 to assign some of their best pilots for duty in the new unit.

The names of the pilots who transferred would in many cases become synonymous with legendary action in P-38s. George Prentice, who had commanded the first P-38 squadron in New Guinea, was chosen to command the new

Maj. Wallace Jordan claimed an Oscar over Wewak on Aug. 2, 1943, for his first victory. Went on to command 9th F.S. and five other scores. Jordan

Fred Champlin's first P-38 in the 431st squadron. Krane

Ken Ladd by one of his original P-38s. Scored first victory over Cape Gloucester on July 29, 1943.　　Krane

Young P-38 pilot Billy Gresham of the 432nd Squadron. P-38 in background was flown by Lt. Charles "Rat" Ratajski.

Grim pilots of the 431st F.S. before their first mission on Aug. 12, 1943. Captain Haning is briefing. Paul Morris is standing far right while Nichols and Smith react to the briefing at far right.

group. Harry Brown and Jack Mankin along with Art Wenige and Frank Nichols came from the 49th Fighter Group to form the new 431st Fighter Squadron. From the 80th Squadron came Danny Roberts and James Ince to help form the nucleus of the 432nd Fighter Squadron.

By May 14, 1943, the 475th came into existence at Amberley Field, Australia, and by the middle of July the group was conducting training flights in preparation for its operational debut in August.

During the period that the 475th Fighter Group was working up to operations, the war in New Guinea increased its tempo; July was an active month for the P-38 units and the pilots who were becoming aces. "Shady" Lane of the 39th Squadron shot down his fifth Japanese aircraft on July 18 when he blasted the wing from an Oscar near Lae. July 21 was a banner day for the 39th when it claimed twelve Japanese over the Ramu Valley and became the first V Fighter Command Squadron to score over 100 victories. Stanley Andrews, Richard Smith and Paul Stanch accounted for five Oscars between them to become aces on the 21st.

By the middle of August the 475th was ready for operations. There was necessarily an element of the prima donna in such a unit that numbered some of the hottest fighter pilots in the V Fighter Command. One of the problems that the group faced in its first missions was the propensity of some pilots to go after individual kills and leave their bomber charges vulnerable to Japanese interceptors. As it was, five American bombers were lost during August.

Tom McGuire was one of the hot pilots who filled the 475th's rolls. Aside from being one of the most talented and aggressive pilots anywhere, he had the reputation of being an unstoppable chatterbox. His incessant talking wearied fellow pilots on the ground and infuriated them in the air when he violated radio discipline. In spite of this unfortunate propensity there is no indication that McGuire ever left a bomber in his charge for the sake of a personal victory.

McGuire claimed three victories in the 475th's second big fight on August 18 and two more during an escort of B-25s over Wewak on August 21. On the latter mission he was leading Blue Flight at 9,000 feet over Wewak when he

Lt. Bill O'Brien, "Pappy" Cline and Fred Champlin before typical 475th F.G. dwelling in August 1943.

via Jeff Ethell

Back row, l to r: Danny Roberts, Leonidas Mathers, Don Hanover, E.C. Krisher (shot down the next day in P-38 behind him), Jess Gidley, Earl Smith, unknown. *Front row:* Harrison Freeman, unknown, Gerald T. Rogers, Frank Tomkins. Every pilot in back row was killed by the beginning of 1944. Photo dated Aug. 20, 1943.

80th Fighter Squadron Association

Lt. Ralph Wire (right) claimed three Japanese with the 9th Fighter Squadron including 2 Zeros over Morobe Harbor on Sept. 6, 1943. He later became an ace with the 449th Fighter Squadron in CBI.

Bob Anderson

Tommy Lynch considers his final score with the 39th Fighter Squadron. He was the only fighter pilot in V Fighter Command to score on Sept. 16, 1943, when he downed a ki-46 Dinah over Hansa Bay for his sixteenth victory.

Lynch's camera gun records his fifteenth victory; a Lily shot down on Sept. 4, 1943. This may have been the first of its type claimed by a V Fighter Command pilot.

C. King

heard a call for help from the P-38 low cover and dived to the rescue. McGuire found a battle going on at 3,000 feet and described the results in his combat report:

> We made a pass at a zeke which I shot down with a 45 [degree] deflection shot at close range. Lt. Lent saw him burn and crash. My second element became separated from me at this time. We then made a pass at a zeke at which Lt. Lent, my wingman, got several good bursts. This plane was seen to crash by Lt. Czarnecki. We were then joined by Lt. Allen and making a steep wingover down to below 1000 feet. Lt. Allen and I got several good bursts at a pair of zekes which were attacking. Both were seen to crash on fire, northeast of Dagua strip.
>
> Turning back to the south we made passes at a twin-engine fighter which I saw Lt. Lent shoot down. The twin-engine fighter had a checkerboard design on the engine cowls and on part of the wings. It crashed into the woods. We climbed up and made passes at another twin-engine fighter (mottled camouflage) at which I got several good bursts, seeing hits by cannon and machine guns around cockpit and right wing root. A small burst of flame appeared but then I lost sight of him as I turned and climbed to avoid a steep hill.
>
> We started for home as we were low on gas. On the way out of the target area I made a few quick passes at a couple of zeros but observed no results. We refueled at Marilinan and continued home.

Nearly fifty Japanese aircraft had been claimed by the 475th in its first three contacts with the enemy. Two of the group's P-38s had been lost and a Distinguished Unit Citation was awarded for the 475th's auspicious combat debut.

Harry Brown had become the first ace of the group when he claimed three Zeros on August 16. With two victories gained over Pearl Harbor in a P-36 and another over the Bismarck Sea with the 9th Squadron he had a total of six confirmed Japanese aircraft. In addition to Tom McGuire, others scoring their fifth victories on August 21 were Danny Roberts, David Allen and Frank Nichols. The result of all the effort.was that airpower from the Japanese base of Wewak was all but erased.

The P-38's star continued to rise in New Guinea during September. Jerry Johnson downed a twin-engine ki-45 Nick over Cape Gloucester for his fifth victory on September 2 and the same day George Welch claimed four victories over Wewak to record his ninth P-38 and 16th total victory.

Two days later the 80th Squadron put up a remarkable performance over the Huon Gulf and accounted for eleven enemy fighters. Ed Cragg and Jay Robbins were trapped by large numbers of Japanese out over the gulf and had to fight their way to safety. Cragg attacked one of about fifteen Zeros that were circling an American destroyer and sent it down in flames. He then outran the angry pack and survived the day with two more victories.

Robbins was even more desperately involved just off the coast of Lae and Salamaua. Robbins had shot up one Zero so badly that its pilot bailed out, but when the P-38 pilot looked around there were about twenty other Japanese fighters on all sides of him. Robbins pointed his nose for shore and fired whenever an enemy plane got in his way. He took some bullet and cannon hits, one of which ripped through his shirt sleeve, but came through the gauntlet, shooting down three more Zeros for sure and possibly two others to keep his life and the new title of ace.

A new record for a V Fighter Command squadron was set on September 22 when the 432nd Squadron was given credit for eighteen victories in a single day. Fred "Squareloop" Harris was leading the 432nd on a cover mission over Finschhafen when a large formation of Betty bombers and Zero fighters threatened the invasion convoy. Harris led the 432nd down on the Japanese formation and personally downed two of the Zeros and a Betty. He had also claimed two Tonys on August 21 and thus claimed his fifth victory. James Ince got a Zero and a Betty for his fourth victory and Zach Dean also scored a Zero and a Betty to begin his scoring.

Two 432nd Lightnings were lost in the battle, including the one flown by Vivian Cloud who bailed out after he downed yet another Betty and Zero. Cloud had dived onto the tail of a Betty at about 5,000 feet and knocked out the tail-cannon with a single burst. He then fired and watched his bullets spatter along the fuselage and wing until the left engine burst into flame and the Betty fell away. As he flew over the wrecked bomber, Cloud saw a Zero straight ahead

James C. Ince, 432nd Sq. ace, claimed a Betty and Zero during the squadron's big day on Sept. 22, 1943. Ince became an ace over Morobe Harbor on Nov. 9, 1943.
Krane

Zach Dean also claimed a Betty and a Zero on Sept. 22, 1943. He shot down his fifth Japanese aircraft on Oct. 24, 1943, over Rabaul.
Krane

-24-

Vivian Cloud at a ceremony which probably preceded his exciting combat of Sept. 22, 1943. He shot down a Tony and an Oscar on Dec. 22, 1943, to claim his fifth victory. Left to right: Lt. Vivian Cloud, Lt. James E. McLaughlin, Lt. Francis Pitonyk and Lt. Bacchus Byrd, Jr.   USAF

and zoomed after the fighter.

The Zero tried a slow roll but Cloud managed to stay with the nimble fighter. Firing intermittently, Cloud set the Zero on fire and watched it crash into the water below. He then tried to help another P-38 under attack, but was jumped by four other Zeros that set one of the P-38's engines on fire. When the fire was reaching the wing tank, Cloud decided to leave and parachuted into the sea. A welcome U.S. destroyer picked him up.

Rabaul, October-November 1943: P-38 ace maker

By the autumn of 1943, Allied planners felt that the eastern end of New Guinea was secure. The Japanese had been unable to check any operation initiated by their adversaries and with the fall of the Lae-Salamaua and Finschhafen areas thousands of Japanese troops were cut off. Fifth Air Force commanders from General Kenney down to squadron leaders were eager to take the offensive.

One obvious item that had to be dealt with was the great bastion at Rabaul on the island of New Britain. With its air and naval facilities in an extremely advantageous position, Rabaul presented a threat to New Guinea and the Solomons and to the line of march to be taken by U.S. naval units in the Central Pacific. MacArthur argued for invasion of Rabaul but was turned down because of the limited availability of equipment and personnel. It was decided to neutralize and bypass the Japanese base.

Fighter-escorted bombing missions were begun by the Fifth Air Force on October 12. The P-38s staged out of Kiriwina Island and took the B-24s through light opposition

Maj. Ed Cragg by his P-38H-1 66506, "Porky II," late September or early October 1943.

-25-

to Simpson Harbor. Although other missions were scheduled for the days that followed, weather prevented operations until October 23.

In the meantime, the Japanese struck back desperately with air raids in the Oro Bay area. Fifty Japanese fighters covering twenty dive-bombers attacked on October 15 and lost about twenty of their number to P-38 interceptors. Grover Fanning claimed a fighter for his seventh victory and Jerry Johnson got two Vals and an Oscar for his sixth victory in the P-38. Hot-flying John O'Neill downed his third Zero for yet another 9th Squadron victory.

The 475th had another good day when it claimed over thirty Japanese. Tom McGuire and Francis Lent teamed up to claim four victories between them. Vincent Elliott, Frank Monk, Paul Morriss and Marion Kirby also scored for the 431st Squadron. Kirby broke into laughter after he shot down his Val because in his excitement he held down the trigger and burned out the gun barrels, causing more tracers to fly off in random directions than to converge on the doomed bomber.

But the most action of the day was seen by the 432nd Squadron. Several flights of the squadron flew through the Japanese formations and a general melee developed. Fred Harris and Vivian Cloud were flying together again and accounted for three of the Vals between them. John Loisel flamed one Zero and exploded another to score his fifth victory. Zach Dean, Billy Gresham and Elliott Summer each scored one victory for the squadron. Two other squadron victories were scored by an interloper from 475th headquarters. Charles MacDonald had purloined a P-38 from the 433rd Squadron and tagged along with the 432nd. He managed to claim two Vals but had to crash-land back at Dobodura.

Two days later another Japanese force was intercepted in the same area and more than twenty other aircraft were claimed. John O'Neill claimed his fourth Zero and Ralph Wandrey got another for his third victory. James Harris made out his combat report claiming only two victories for the 9th Squadron but a recent Air Force study credits him with three, which would make him an ace of the 9th Squadron.

Only three P-38s were lost in the battle. One of these was flown by rising star Tom McGuire. McGuire had dropped his belly tanks and followed Marion Kirby into a head-on attack at about fifteen Zeros, which were slightly above the P-38 altitude of 23,000 feet. McGuire fired at one Zero on the right of the formation and saw him roll and fall away smoking. McGuire climbed to regain altitude and went to the rescue of another P-38 beset by Zeros. McGuire was jumped by four Zeros and the chase was on again.

The battle went on, McGuire taking a shot at one Zero then skidding or diving violently to avoid another Zero. The men in the Japanese fighters were good; there was some speculation that they were the old Tainan Air Corps, which

Lt. Paul C. Murphey, one of the last aces of the 80th F.S., scored his second victory when he downed a Hamp over Kabanga Bay, Rabaul on Oct. 24, 1943.　　Louis Schriber

Ed Cragg in the cockpit of his P-38. Note the early type control wheel which caused some discomfort during long flights.

Lt. J.W. Harris originally claimed two victories over Oro Bay on Oct. 17, 1943.　　Krane

n. JONES   MAJ.   CAPT.   CAPT.   LT.   LT.
                                                     CHILDS   HOMER

had boasted the greatest aces of the Japanese Navy in the Pacific.

Whoever they were, they nearly spelled the end for Tom McGuire. When he flew his P-38 straight and level long enough to shoot another Zero off the tail of a P-38, several Zeros tacked onto the tail of his P-38 and would not let him go. Cannon shells and machine-gun bullets mercilessly riddled his engines and cockpit, tearing his radio apart and setting fire to an entire engine and tail-boom assembly. McGuire noticed in fascination that a 7.7-mm bullet had passed through his wrist but that there was no pain.

It was clearly time to abandon the stricken P-38 and McGuire scrambled to clear the cockpit. He managed to get halfway out but was then shocked to find that not only was he caught on the jagged wreckage of the cockpit but that he was blinded by an inky blackness. Quickly he realized that his oxygen mask had wrapped itself around his eyes in the rushing slipstream. He tore the thing away and frantically ripped himself free into space.

In an instant he was seized by another bit of horror when he discovered that his ripcord handle was gone. Wrapping the frayed end of the wire around his hand, McGuire gave it a determined yank and was greatly relieved when the parachute canopy finally opened only moments before he hit the sea.

He was dismayed once again to find that his life raft was damaged and would only partially open. Life had been uncertain for young Tom McGuire but now he couldn't be sure whether Americans, Japanese or the sharks would get to him first. Luckily, he only had to spend about 45 minutes in the water before a patrol boat picked him up and deposited him in the sick bay of the PT tender HILO. McGuire's luck even permitted the crew of the patrol boat to witness the entire air battle and confirm three Zeros shot down for him!

Once the offensive against Rabaul resumed there was a terrible momentum created in the ranks of the V Fighter Command. On October 23 eighteen Japanese fighters were claimed by P-38s sweeping ahead of the B-24s. Vincent Elliott of the 431st Squadron was credited with two Zeros and was the first P-38 pilot to become an ace over Rabaul. Jerry Johnson also claimed a Zero and Danny Roberts downed two others to begin a remarkable string of five Japanese fighters downed over Rabaul. Paul Stanch of the 39th Squadron found himself in a covey of Oscars (contrary to wartime Japanese reports, there were many Oscars stationed at Rabaul in the autumn of 1943) with one of his P-38's engines streaming coolant. He reacted vigorously and shot his way out, claiming one of the Oscars for his tenth and final victory.

The P-38s were back the next day escorting B-25s. No fewer than forty Japanese were claimed by the escort and five P-38 pilots became aces. The 432nd Squadron was racing in low over the water near Rabaul with nineteen P-38s when it was jumped from above by an estimated fifty Zeros. Six Japanese fighters paid the price when the 432nd responded quickly. Billy Gresham claimed a Zero and Zach Dean downed another Zero and a Hamp to register their fifth victories. Calvin Wire of the 475th's 433rd Squadron also downed two Zeros for his initiation into acedom.

John O'Neill and Ralph Wandrey were flying over the sea near Cape Gazelle when they ran into another Japanese formation. Wandrey downed an Oscar for his fourth victory and O'Neill shot two Zeros to pieces to join the ranks of the aces.

Jay Robbins continued his remarkable scoring when he destroyed four Hamps, one of which appeared to be attempting to ram Robbins. Corky Smith scored another Zero for the 80th Squadron and thus was the fifth P-38 pilot to become an ace over Rabaul on October 24. The combat report for the day reflects the difficulty faced by combat pilots

Allen Hill (right) was one of the P-38 pilots who rose in reputation during the Rabaul operations. He claimed a Zero on Oct. 29, 1943, two more Zeros and a probable on Nov. 2nd, and yet another on Nov. 7 to become an ace. 80th F.S.

Front port quarter of Hill's P-38J early in 1944. 80th F.S.

over Rabaul:

80th Fighter Squadron
Combat Mission Report

A. Mission No. 225 24 Oct. 43. 16 P-38s

B. Escort B-25s to Rapopo, New Britain

C. TO: 0645 - Land Dobodura 0800 - TO: Dobodura 0835 Over target 1130 to 1150 at 0 - 11,000 feet

D. 10 Hamps and 1 Zeke definite - 1 Hamp probable Our losses: 5 P-38s damaged, one of which crash-landed at Kiriwina. 1 pilot, Maj. Edward Cragg, slightly wounded in right arm.

E. Approximately 40-50 Hamps and Zekes intercepted when in vicinity of Kabanga Bay on approach at approx. 1130 hrs.

F. Enemy was first sighted when several Hamps were seen attacking B-25s in vicinity of Kabanga Bay. Others were sighted above up to 10,000 feet. Combat ensued and ranged from ground level to 10,000 feet. Enemy stayed in pairs or more. All enemy airplanes were painted black and seemed to have especially good pilots.

G. Nil (anti-aircraft)

H. Gun camera shots

I. One B-25 seen to crash in water just off Cape Wanata, shot down by enemy fighters.

J. Scattered to broken clouds over target area and en route.

K. 1 P-38 landed at 0935, mechanical trouble; 1 P-38 landed at 1000, mechanical trouble; 1 P-38 landed at 1045, mechanical trouble; 1 P-38 had mechanical trouble at Dobodura and is still there. Did not take part in the mission. 1 P-38 crash-landed at Kiriwina after mission, pilot uninjured, plane was damaged in combat. 3 P-38s were damaged in combat and remained at Kiriwina. 1 P-38 had mechanical trouble and remained at Kiriwina.

L. 24 belly tanks dropped. Six planes expended 2320 cal. 50s and 527 20 mms.

October 25 saw another B-24 escort but most of the fighters had to turn back when weather fronts suddenly moved in. Only two flights of the 432nd Squadron flying high cover managed to climb to 27,500 feet and stay with the bombers. Charles MacDonald managed to intervene with his seven fighters when a number of Zeros and Tonys appeared and even claimed a Zero for his third victory.

Weather again delayed Fifth Air Force operations until October 29 when sixty-two P-38s shepherded the B-24s once more to Rabaul. Ralph Wandrey of the 9th Squadron and John Smith of the 433rd claimed an Oscar and a Zero to become the latest P-38 aces over the Japanese base. A few

Marion Kirby scored his final three confirmed victories over Rabaul. The first was a Hamp on Oct. 23 and the last two were Zeros on Nov. 2, 1943. Kirby was known as a tiger in both the 80th and 431st Squadrons for his enthusiasm in combat.   Dennis Cooper

"Screwy" Louis Schriber who claimed three of the 80th Fighter Sq. probables on Nov. 2, 1943. He went on to claim six confirmed victories later in the war.   Schriber

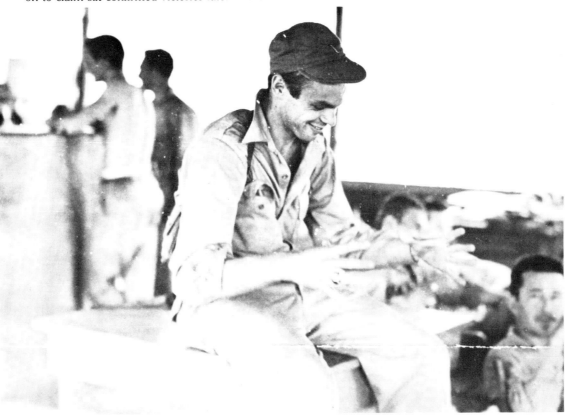

minutes before either one of these pilots made their score, Charles King downed two Oscars and was the last P-38 ace of the 39th. King had experimentally installed color film in his gun camera and obtained impressively clear films of the demise of the two Oscars.

November 2 brought a climax to the assault on Rabaul and became known in the Fifth Air Force as "Bloody Tuesday." Nearly every P-38 in the Fifth Air Force inventory was sent up to protect the B-25s that would sweep in at low level to bomb the facilities and ships in Simpson Harbor. The P-38s of the 39th and 80th Squadrons came in at low altitudes to clear the way. The 39th was at a somewhat higher level and encountered only one Japanese fighter. This was quickly dispatched.

Meanwhile, below a cloud layer, P-38s of the 80th Squadron ran into a hornet's nest of Zeros and Tonys along with a smaller formation of Hamps and Vals. John Jones destroyed one of the Hamps for his last victory and Ed Degraffenreid got a Zero for his sixth and last score. Allen Hill downed two other Zeros to register his fourth victory and five other Hamps and Zeros fell to 80th P-38s. However, two squadron Lightnings were also shot down into Simpson Harbor.

Lightnings of the 9th Squadron and 475th Fighter Group, closely guarding the B-25s, arrived over the target at about 1:30 p.m. Jerry Johnson immediately turned his P-38 into the path of attacking fighters and downed two Zeros. Al Lewelling also shot down an attacking Oscar for his first 9th Squadron victory.

The 475th had a warm reception over the entrance of Simpson Harbor when Japanese warships blocked the way and fired at any P-38 or B-25 unlucky enough to come into range. In the rough fighting eleven Japanese fighters were credited to the 431st Squadron, a Zero falling to Lowell Lutton for his fifth victory. Arthur Wenige claimed two Zeros for his fifth claim and fourth victory with the P-38. Grover

Gholson also downed two Japanese fighters for his fifth victory, fourth with the P-38s of the 432nd Squadron.

Fred Champlin claimed two Zeros for the 431st Fighter Squadron. One of the Japanese that Champlin claimed was hot on the tail of Marion Kirby, who had himself just shot down two other Zeros to be counted a P-38 ace. When Kirby could finally take a look around, he was startled to see the sides of the volcanic hills in the harbor alive with anti-aircraft fire; the American raiders were so low that gunfire was directed downward upon them. For the forty or so claimed victories, the American force had lost eight B-25s and nine P-38s, one of which was piloted by brand-new P-38 ace Lowell Lutton.

In the days ahead, the Thirteenth Air Force and Navy and Marine air units would carry on the assault that finally neutralized Rabaul as a base in March 1944. With the last V Fighter Command missions to Rabaul during November, Allen Hill and Art Wenige both scored their fifth P-38 victories on November 7. Two days before, Dick Bong was leading a flight of the 9th Squadron over Rabaul, when he observed two very dark-colored Zeros. His wingman, Lieutenant Nutter, watched as Bong quickly flamed both Japanese aircraft. The score for Richard Ira Bong now stood at twenty-one confirmed victories, more than any other U.S. Army pilot at the time. General Kenney had promised that he could go home on furlough as soon as he reached the twenty mark and Bong readily accepted the offer.

The war on the New Guinea front had certainly passed onto the offensive for the Allies. With one Japanese base after another falling, the outcome was becoming clearer. Japanese and American airmen had taken the brunt of their respective nations' competition in the Pacific and they had performed with courage and determination. In the end, however, a decided technical advantage had swung the balance against the Japanese.

P-38s of the 80th F.S. escort a B-25 of the 3rd Bomb Group to Rabaul on Nov. 2, 1943. Pilots of the P-38s are reputed to be Major Cragg in A and Cy Homer in V. V was Homer's early P-38 named "Cotton Duster."

Chapter 4
Fifth Air Force from Rabaul to VJ Day

Danny Roberts' P-38 as it appeared about the time of his death.

*A*s SOON AS THE FIFTH AIR FORCE ended its participation in the reduction of Rabaul, its attention was turned to the northern coast of New Guinea. Saidor and Alexishafen became immediate targets in the leapfrog tactics that saw Allied units attack Japanese bases which then became points for new attacks on targets farther to the northwest.

Attrition at Rabaul had not been excessive for the P-38s. Less than 20 had been lost to all causes, although, for whatever reason, the Japanese had claimed well over 100 Lightnings shot down during October and November. But, supportable as the losses may have been, General Kenney was forced to re-equip two P-38 squadrons, the venerable 9th and 39th, with P-47s. Within six months the pilots of the 9th would rejoice when once again they received the highly valued P-38, but the 39th would nevermore set records in the Lockheed fighter.

On one of the first missions to Alexishafen flown on November 9, V Fighter Command endured yet another loss. Danny Roberts and his wingman Dale Meyer had dived hard onto the tails of several Hamps and Oscars and Roberts sent one of the Japanese fighters down in flames. He was chasing yet another Japanese when the enemy pilot made a sharp turn. Although Roberts was good enough to follow the Japanese fighter at low altitude, Meyer simply could not duplicate the maneuver and crashed full-speed into Roberts' P-38. Both aircraft fell the scant 200 feet to earth and burst into flames.

The death of Danny Roberts was not the last mishap to befall V Fighter Command P-38s at the end of 1943. One bad mission was flown by the 80th Squadron on December 22. Seventeen P-38s of the squadron were close to their objective while they were escorting B-25s to Wewak. Eight Japanese Tony fighters came out of the sun through broken clouds to jump the last flight of P-38s and sent one down smoking. Another of the 80th's flights turned to the aid of its comrades and engaged the Japanese. By this time other Tonys and Oscars entered the fray and engaged the entire 80th. Corky Smith downed one of the Oscars but had one of his engines damaged in the process and ran for the deck all alone, managing to elude the Japanese after a great deal of effort.

Jennings Myers was credited with one Tony on this mission but disappeared, never to be seen again. His P-38 was observed crash-landing off Karau Lagoon, near the mouth of the Sepik River. He was able to get out of his plane, swim ashore and take cover in the jungle but then apparently was lost. The Tony was his fifth victory. Myers was an old hand in the squadron who would undoubtedly have rotated home within the next few weeks.

Five Japanese aircraft were credited to the 80th pilots but they paid heavily with two P-38s lost and two others heavily damaged. Another costly mission was flown by the 80th on December 26 over Borgen Bay, New Britain, during the invasion by U.S. Marines. A force of about twenty-five dive-bombers covered by fifty Zeros was intercepted by several formations of P-38s including the 80th Squadron. Ten victories were claimed, including the last victory for Ed Cragg, reportedly one of the formidable ki-44 Tojos, but two more P-38s were lost with one pilot killed. That was Cragg himself.

With the coming of the new year, 1944, good news arrived for V Fighter Command. Early in the year Tommy Lynch returned and was assigned to the command headquarters. Lynch had been understandably promoted to lieutenant colonel and promised renewed leadership for American fighter operations in New Guinea. Dick Bong also returned and continued to buoy the spirits of Fifth Air Force

Dick West on his P-40N sometime at the end of 1943. West scored six victories in the P-40 and then eight more in the P-38 between June and November 1944.   West

Dick West and other members of the 35th Fighter Squadron. This unit had the best record in the V Fighter Command with the P-40 at the end of 1943 and beginning of 1944. They also did well with the P-38.

West

Jess Gidley and Jennings Myers of the 80th Fighter Squadron. Both would be lost by the end of 1943, Myers just as he claimed his fifth victory.   USAF

Billy Gresham's P-38J-5 s/n 42-67147 "Black Market Babe" sometime late in January after he had claimed a Zero over Wewak for his last victory.   Krane

air crews with his winning personality and casual confidence in aerial combat.

Lynch and Bong began flying together much as they had during the early days of P-38 deployment in New Guinea. Bong was a mustang in combat and needed some sort of tempering. Lynch offered that control and Bong was only too glad to follow his lead. The irrepressible and talented Bong considered Lynch one of his best friends and respected his leadership.

By the time they started flying together, Bong had twenty-one air victories and Lynch had seventeen. Capt. Eddie Rickenbacker of World War I fame had been to the theater on a visit and promised a case of whiskey to the first pilot who broke his record of twenty-six aerial victories. By the first of March only one other pilot came close to challenging Bong and Lynch in the race to beat the magic number. Neel Kearby had twenty-one victories with his P-47 and was pushing hard for top honors. Tom McGuire had been in the hospital for several weeks since the mission of October 17, 1943. His score stood at thirteen. He did not learn his lesson, though, for on the first mission after he left the hospital, McGuire waded into a flock of Vals over Borgen Bay and shot down three of them.

But Bong and Lynch were able to pick and choose the missions that they flew and did well with their choices. On March 3, over Tadji, the pair ran into a formation of bombers covered by Tony fighters.

The two Americans coordinated their attacks closely

and as a result Bong was credited with two Sally bombers and Lynch now had a total of nineteen confirmed when he downed two Tonys. Two days later, the two P-38 aces were at 17,000 feet over Wewak when they dropped tanks to attack a formation of Oscars almost 15,000 feet below. Bong covered Lynch's firing passes, which netted one Oscar confirmed and one damaged for his twentieth and final victory.

While Lynch and Bong were in the Tadji area on March 9, they happened to find some Japanese luggers offshore and decided to go down and strafe. Lynch's plane took a hit and in quick succession, a propeller flew off the P-38, Lynch hurtled out of the cockpit and the fighter disappeared in a bright explosion. Bong flew around the area for a time, looking for some sign of his friend's survival but all hope vanished. Bong was depressed by Lynch's loss and was ordered out of the air for a few days.

By the time Bong reported once more for duty, the Fifth Air Force was ready to assault the last big Japanese bastion on the north coast of New Guinea at Hollandia. From the end of March until the middle of April, the 8th and 475th fighter groups would deal roughly with Japanese interceptors that tried to interfere with the bombers.

On March 30 and 31 the two fighter groups accounted for no less than twenty-four Japanese fighters. On the third day of April, another twenty-four Japanese fell, including Dick Bong's twenty-fifth victory and a remarkable triple destruction of Oscars for the 475th's Joseph Forster on his first combat.

Louis Schriber by his P-38J sometime in the early spring of 1944.

One ace of the 80th Fighter Squadron did not have so spectacular a victory but the record of Kenneth Ladd is impressive in its consistent effectiveness. Scoring for the first time against a Dinah on July 29, 1943, Ladd steadily increased his score until he claimed what was probably his tenth Japanese aircraft on April 3 over Hollandia. He was leading the fifth and last flight of the squadron when the 80th dropped tanks to engage Oscars that were attacking the B-24s:

> I spotted an Oscar at 12 o'clock to me and proceeded to give chase. Closing in to about 200 yards I let loose with a long burst and saw several of my cannon shells explode on the Oscar's fuselage. My wingman saw this plane go down in flames. My next shot was at another Oscar who was taking full advantage of cloud protection. My fire hit this plane, but I saw him fly away, so I can make no claims. I had one other shot which was at a Nip going straight down. Again I saw my fire strike the plane, but no further results were observed. Today the enemy seemed more eager to fight than in the previous two combats, but still they are very much on the defensive.

April 12 was the red-letter day for breaking Rickenbacker's record as the 80th Fighter Squadron claimed another eight Japanese plus a probable that was later confirmed. Corky Smith claimed his eleventh and final victory when he got another Oscar over the coast of Hollandia. Jay Robbins stopped another pair of Tonys for his seventeenth and eighteenth victories. Burnell Adams shot down an Oscar and a Tony and had the distinction of witnessing Dick

Bong surpass the record. Bong had the privilege of flying with just about any group he pleased and sometimes flew with the pugnacious "Headhunters," as the 80th Fighter Squadron was known. He claimed two definites and one probable that was confirmed after the mission. Adams' combat report records the fall of at least one of Bong's victories:

> I made one pass at an Oscar in a thin cloud that you couldn't see all the way thru, but could see a plane in range. I drove up on this Oscar and gave it a long burst and saw my 50's and cannons breaking on it. It turned sharply and the next thing I know he's sitting on my tail firing at me. I don't know how the hell he did it, but he did it damned fast. I dived out of the cloud expecting my wingman to knock him off, but I had lost my wingman and had to shake him myself. I shoved everything forward and nosed her over. I began to pull away from him and he broke away and went back to the clouds. I followed him back and Captain Bong was making passes on another Oscar. I didn't observe his results on this Nip because I saw another drop out of the cloud over to my left and turned into him. I didn't get within range of him; I lost him. I saw another Oscar down about 1,000 feet, made a pass and saw my bursts hitting and exploding, but the Oscar kept flying. Captain Bong made a head-on pass at him and didn't score, so I drove right up on his tail and gave him a long burst. He was in flames and I had oil all over my windshield from him so I broke down and away from him. Captain Bong saw him explode and go in. I went on over the hill and the next thing I saw was Captain Bong driving right up the tail of an Oscar right on the deck. He gave a short burst and the Oscar hit the water and sank rapidly . . .

John Loisel's P-38 sometime after January 1944.

-34-

80th F.S. Area seen over the nose of Paul Murphey's P-38.

Decoration on Ralph Wandrey's P-47. Wandrey was so displeased with the decision to equip the 9th Fighter Squadron with the P-47 that he claimed he called his flight to attention whenever a P-38 flew over in reverence for a *real* airplane. Wandrey earned the nickname "Ironass" when he threatened to court martial any wingman who left him alone in a combat area.
Wandrey

Frank Lent on his P-38J-15 "Trigger Mortis" in the spring of 1944. Greg Morris

Lent and McGuire after an awards ceremony. McGuire is wearing the Purple Heart he won when he was shot down on Oct. 17, 1943.   Krane

58th F.G. crewman Joe Papatola examining Jandina III while it was being repaired after being crash landed by Robbins at Saidor on May 7, 1944.

Papatola via Charles Mayer

P-38 of Zach Dean. The natural metal finish on V Fighter Command P-38s began to appear about the middle of March 1944. Dean scored his sixth and seventh victories over Wewak on Dec. 22, 1943, when he claimed two Oscars.

Robbins leading the 80th Fighter Squadron on a mission in Jandina III.

Burnell Adams in W leading an 80th Fighter Squadron mission off the ground. T is in the trail. This mission was about the same time that Bong broke Eddie Rickenbacker's WWI record of 26 aerial victories.

Krane

Dick Bong flew 80th F.S. P-38J-15 s/n 42-104012 "Downbeat" on April 1, 1944. Crew chief Sam Scher remembers meeting Bong just before the mission, exchanging a few comments before the mission and talking to Bong when the mission was aborted. Bong made some complimentary remarks about the maintenance of Scher's P-38 and Scher never saw Bong again.

Scher

Ken Ladd about the time that he scored his tenth victory, the Oscar he downed over Hollandia on April 3, 1944.

80th F.S. Association

Paul Murphey scored his fourth victory with the 80th Fighter Squadron over Hollandia on March 30, 1944.

Schriber

With at least twenty-seven confirmed victories to his credit, Bong was once again sent home as a symbol of American successes in the air.

Since he was a teetotaler, Bong had promised the prizes of liquor to his thirsty squadronmates. Spirits were dashed in more ways than one shortly thereafter when groups like the Women's Christian Temperance Union protested such corruption of American youth. Bong readily accepted Coca-Cola as a substitute but the pilots of the P-38s who were denied the prize were dismal at the prospect of somewhat drier air combat.

And the air combat, and its dangers, did continue. During an escort of PBY air-sea rescue operations on May 7, Jay Robbins ran into some mechanical difficulties and could not lower his landing gear. After some hectic dueling with severe weather over his home base he flew to the Saidor area with minimum fuel. Robbins relates the subsequent events in a letter written in 1974:

. . . . As we were attempting to return to base at Nadzab, severe weather developed over the Markham River Valley and the northern coast of New Guinea. . . . After getting into the Saidor area with minimum fuel, I was advised that the runways and taxiways at Saidor were blocked by other aircraft. . . . Thus, I had no runway to land on and insufficient fuel to proceed to any other suitable

landing strip . . . After approximately 15-20 minutes of attempting to lower the gear, it became obvious that I would not be able to do so. [I] noticed a very short strip (dirt) surrounded by high trees just a few miles northwest of Saidor.

. . . . In preparation for the belly landing, I had buckled myself in as tightly as I could, so the only injury I sustained during the landing was a fairly deep cut on my forehead from the gunsight. The airplane skidded past the end of the strip and across a small ditch. Most of the damage to the P-38 occurred when I hit the ditch. The skid was fairly short (400-500 feet) and fairly smooth—although the noise of the props hitting was louder than I had expected. Fortunately, there was no fire—even so, I exited the aircraft as quickly as possible with some help from people who were close by during the landing.

Lightnings with Long Legs

Charles MacDonald was commanding the 475th during the summer of 1944 when a special visitor showed up at the group's new base at freshly won Hollandia. Charles Lindbergh was no longer the daring young flyer but he had retained the keen mind that successfully dealt with the problems of flying alone across the Atlantic. One of the difficulties that Lindbergh had helped solve that now interested P-38

McGuire's P-38H-5 s/n 42-66817 "Pudgy II" with 17 victory marks. If all the victories were confirmed, this photo would have been taken in mid-May 1944—a late period for camouflaged early marks of the P-38.

Pilots of the 80th by Jandina IV on Owi.

pilots in the Pacific was that of extending fighter range. When Lindbergh appeared at Hollandia with promised benefits for the 475th, MacDonald was especially glad to see him.

Lindbergh was allowed to fly with the 475th and, in spite of Fifth Air Force disapproval, MacDonald even allowed Lindbergh on combat missions. He almost regretted his permissiveness, however, when on at least one mission he was obliged to chase a Japanese fighter away from the Lone Eagle's Lightning. But Lindbergh was no defenseless novice—he shot down a ki-51 Sonia reconnaissance aircraft on July 28.

Headquarters finally found out about the caper and put an end to the combat activities of civilian Lindbergh. For his part in allowing Lindbergh to fly into danger, MacDonald was sent home on punitive leave and the 475th was led during the next two months by one of his few close confidants, Meryl Smith. Actually, MacDonald couldn't have cared less since he had a baby son at home whom he had not yet seen and there was plenty of time to finish his impressive record.

Lindbergh's visit did have a decidedly positive effect on the V Fighter Command units graced by his presence. He taught the pilots how to properly use their manifold pressure for economical fuel consumption; many P-47s and P-38s were now doubling their effective combat range. While the P-38 could fly from its base to a point approximately 525 miles away before Lindbergh's visit, it could now fly missions well over 800 miles.

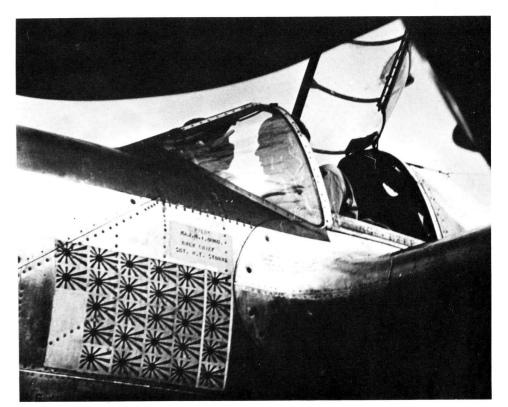

Charles A. Lindbergh seated in Dick Bong's P-38 after Bong had broken Rickenbacker's record. Mid-1944.

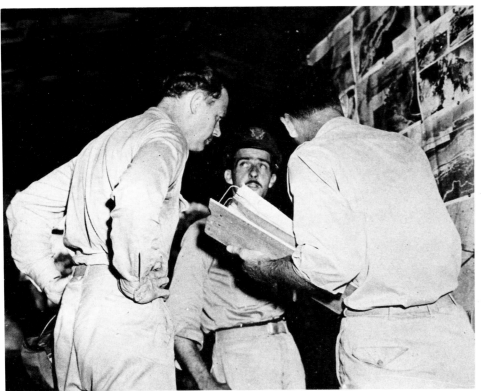

Lindbergh and McGuire during the period that they flew missions together in the summer of 1944.

Anderson

One of the first missions to benefit from the extended range was the operation to the oil targets on Balikpapan, more than 800 miles from bases on Morotai. On October 10, P-38s and P-47s were able to escort the B-24 s all the way and claimed eighteen interceptors confirmed shot down.

Wallace Jordan, who became known as "Major Stitch" after he suffered a head cut in a jeep accident, was the commander of the 9th Fighter Squadron and personally led the unit over Balikpapan on October 10. One member of his flight was Dick Bong, who had returned from home as a gunnery instructor and went along to see how his students benefited from his teaching. When the flight dived on a Nick twin-engine fighter far below, Bong proved his skill by setting fire to the Japanese aircraft with two well-aimed bursts.

Jordan and Warren Curton ran into a formation of

Lt. John S. Dunaway by his P-38J-15 #27 in the summer of 1944.   Krane

Oscars a few minutes later and each pilot shot down one of the Japanese fighters. On the way out of the Balikpapan area, Jordan sighted a dark green twin-engine aircraft and identified it as a J1n1 "Irving" night-fighter; he flamed it for his fifth confirmed victory. Bong also claimed a Zero on his way out for victory number thirty.

October 1944 also saw the beginning of a tragic period for the pilots of P-38 fighters in the Pacific area. Billy Gresham was a promising P-38 pilot who had claimed his sixth victory when he downed a Zero over Wewak on January 18. In early October he took up a brand new P-38 for a test flight over Biak when apparently something went wrong and he was forced to bail out. When searchers found the wreckage they also found the body of Gresham in the partially opened parachute. Just ten days after Gresham disappeared another P-38 pilot, Lee Everhart, died when his P-38 crashed on October 12.

Another high-scoring P-38 ace was killed on the second mission to Balikpapan. Ken Ladd had been an old hand with the 80th Fighter Squadron and scored steadily from July 1943 until he downed an Oscar over Hollandia on April 3, 1944, for his tenth victory. He agreed to take over command of the 36th Fighter Squadron when that unit converted to the P-38 and led it with enthusiasm.

On October 14, Ladd took off in a flight comprised of Col. Earl Dunham, Ladd, Colonel Beck and Jay Robbins. The four P-38s were off at 7 a.m. and arrived over the target a little after eleven. Robbins and Beck had aborted the mission by the time five Oscars were sighted below. Dunham followed Ladd in a dive on the little fighters and watched while he set fire to one Oscar. The Japanese pilot bailed out.

Dunham then observed Ladd fire at another Japanese fighter; it began to smoke fiercely and went into a steep glide. In the twisting dogfight Dunham attacked another Oscar and lost sight of Ladd. When he failed to reach Ladd by radio, Dunham turned for home. He learned from other

Scoreboard of Dunaway's P-38 in November 1944.
Krane

witnesses that Ladd had flown into yet another group of Japanese fighters and was last seen in trouble, trying to reach safety with one engine trailing smoke. Ladd was given credit for two fighters—an Oscar and a Tojo—but never returned from the Balikpapan mission.

Other P-38 aces fared better that day. Joe Forster and Meryl Smith of the 475th downed a Hamp and a Zero. Forster had the distinction afterward of setting a world record by flying from Balikpapan on Borneo to Morotai with one of his P-38's engines shut down. Tom McGuire tagged along unofficially with the 49th Fighter Group and claimed an Oscar, a Tojo and a Hamp to register his twenty-fourth victory while Jerry Johnson downed an Oscar and a Tojo to tally thirteen victories with the V Fighter Command. Colonel MacDonald was furious with McGuire for his unauthorized flight and the usually brash young ace withered under his commander's chewing-out.

Dick Bong, Wallace Jordan, Edward B. Howes and Warren Curton after the Oct. 10, 1944, mission to Balikpapan.   Howes

A major milestone in the Pacific war was reached when American troops invaded Leyte in the Philippines on October 20. By the 27th, personnel of the V Fighter Command were coming ashore and the first P-38s were on Philippine soil. The 49th Fighter Group, which had converted entirely to the P-38 by September, was based at Tacloban.

Twilight of Glory: Climax in the Philippines

It was a young second lieutenant of the 7th Fighter Squadron who, on October 29, scored the 49th Fighter Group's 500th aerial victory. Milden Mathre took off with five other P-38s from Tacloban during a patrol on squadron mission number 365-B. A single Oscar was sighted above the 7th Squadron formation and the P-38s immediately climbed above the fighter and started a diving attack. The Oscar also dived and zoomed quickly enough to cause the first P-38 element to overshoot. Mathre, however, was the number four man in pursuit and in a perfect position to fire on the enemy aircraft and send it down in flames. It was the first victory of five for Mathre, the last being a Zero downed over Clark Field on New Year's Day, 1945.

Indeed, the period in which Mathre gained his victories was perhaps the swansong for P-38s in World War II. Between November 1 and the end of 1944 about 400 victories were gained by V Fighter Command Lightnings over the Philippines. Total victories for the command's P-38s during the entire war amounted to just over 1,350, giving some idea of the importance that this late period had in the history of P-38 operations.

But the victories were not without their price. John Dunaway had two victories to his credit on November 6 when he was part of a 36th Fighter Squadron formation over Fabrica Airdrome on Negros Island. Fifteen Japanese aircraft appeared directly above the formation and by the time the fight was over eight Japanese had fallen in flames, with Dunaway responsible for two Zeros, a Tony and a Kate. One other victory, gained on November 14, was credited to him before he was lost over Kaohe Bay while he was on a routine flight and his wing caught a wave during a low turn.

Francis Lent had been Tom McGuire's wingman during the first days of the 475th's operations and had scored eleven victories by the end of March, 1944. As happened to all combat pilots, Lent became burnt-out and had to step down from operations. But the love of aviation still glowed in the young pilot and he took the chance on December 1 to test fly a new photo-reconnaissance F-6D Mustang. Something malfunctioned and Lent crashed to his death. Another 475th Fighter Group ace was lost just a few days later when Meryl Smith, who only a few weeks before had stepped down as group commander after MacDonald's return, disappeared on December 7 during a mission over Ormoc Bay.

Other P-38 aces were more fortunate. Jack Purdy of the 433rd Squadron crash-landed in a Philippine forest and walked back to American hands. A quiet-voiced young pilot from Wisconsin who had hundreds of combat hours and at least seven victories in P-38s went down over Clark Field on Christmas day. Bob Aschenbrener also returned a few days later and was fortunate enough to survive the war.

Perry Dahl was one of the most remarkably fortunate when he returned after going down over Ormoc Bay on November 10. Known as "Pee Wee" Dahl, he had joined the 432nd Squadron on the same day that Joe Forster came along—October 27, 1943. While Forster did not officially score against the enemy until April, the bright-eyed and broad-smiling Dahl knocked down a Zero on his first mission. He nearly came to grief early. During a mission on November 19, 1943, the coolant in both of his P-38's engines began to stream and he reached a friendly landing strip only in the nick of time.

Dahl had already claimed a Tony on November 10, 1944, when he collided with a wingman and was forced to leave his stricken Lightning. He landed in the water and nervously looked around for help but saw only Japanese ships and aircraft. At one point an enemy destroyer cruised by slowly and Dahl did his best to resemble the coconuts floating in the vicinity. Merciful darkness fell and the enemy ships withdrew, allowing the soaked American pilot to make for shore. Happily, Dahl was able to contact Philippine guerrillas and spent a month in the fashion of a privateer. On December 10 he walked into the 432nd camp with a pet monkey on his shoulder. By early June 1945, Dahl was one of the lucky pilots to be rotated home for good.

Other P-38 aces were finishing their records and returning home. Jay Robbins flamed an Oscar over Negros Island while he was flying with the 36th Squadron on November 14 for his twenty-second victory. A few days later he was on his way home. Dick Bong ended his record in December with an Oscar on the 15th and another on the 17th. With forty confirmed victories, he was on his way home by December 29 as the greatest American ace of the war.

One of Bong's friends in the 9th Fighter Squadron had a surge of victories over the Philippines during November. Cheatham Gupton claimed that "all hell broke loose over the Philippines in November" and proved it by claiming two Vals on the first of the month and two Oscars on the 16th. He entered into a friendly rivalry with his squadronmate Leslie Nelson, who also had four victories, over which man would

get the fifth victory first. Gupton downed an Oscar over Tacloban on November 26 and chortled with glee as Nelson responded with mock invective when brand-new ace Cheatham W. Gupton announced his fifth victory over an open radio channel.

Capt. Alfred Lewelling, Lieutenant Gupton and Lieutenant Hoek on Mindoro.   Gupton

Lt. Charles B. Ray by his P-38J-15. Ray became an ace on Dec. 29, 1944 when he claimed a Dinah and a Zero over Mindoro. These victories were some of the last in World War II for the 80th F.S.

On wing: (l to r) B.M. Krankowitz, R.C. Kirtland, D. Curl, R.A. Swift, F.W. Helterline, W.D. Curton, D.W. Fisher, I.I. Curley, W.C. Boyd, R.D. Campbell, H.H. Norton, L.D. Nelson, M. Mathre. *On ground:* (l to r) R. Morrissey, G. Walker, R. DeHaven, W. Drier, G. Smerchek, C.A. Estes, W.R. Jordan, R.I.Bong, G.R. Johnson, A.B. Lewelling, C.I. McElroy, R.W. Wood, W.F. Williams, J.I. Forgey, T. Smith, C.W. Gupton (Gupton) Everybody in the 9th F.S. who wasn't flying that day gathered for this picture. Date is late in November 1944 when 49th F.G. was approaching 600 victories.

Cy Homer by his P-38 late in 1944.   Homer

Cy Homer and Corky Smith by "Corky IV." Photo dated May 1944.

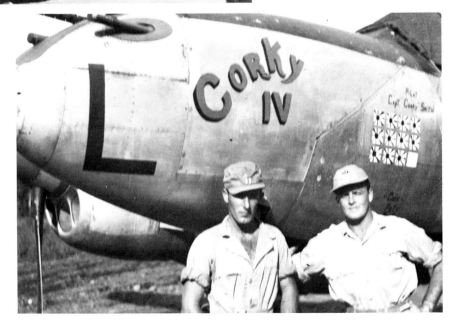

-44-

Bob Aschenbrener and Bill Drier also had good fortune during a patrol west of Tacloban on November 24, as evinced by Aschenbrener's encounter report:

. . . . Leaving our second element above as cover, we attacked the Tony. I fired at him from directly astern and a slight angle of deflection and my bursts completely blew his whole tail section and part of his right wing off. We attempted to reform with the rest of the flight [but] sighted more enemy aircraft at that time. We observed a formation of about 20 bombers and 20 fighters heading southeast toward Tacloban at about 18000'. As we maneuvered, we lost them in the sun but spotted other fighters milling about at the same altitude just west of the strip area. We made contact just inland from the bay. Captain DRIER attacked a 4 ship flight of Zekes and I went after a Zeke flying singly apart from the others. After [I had fired] several bursts, the Zeke crashed between Patong and Jaro. The Zeke Captain DRIER fired at from an angle of deflection, began to smoke heavily and crashed inland near San Miguel. I then made a pass at a Tony who fell off into a right dive and Captain DRIER observed it catch fire and the pilot bail out. I fired at the remaining Tony in their element of two and only one of my guns would work. From a distance of 50 yards, I fired a single burst and pulled up. Lieutenant FRANKS of the 7th Squadron, one (sic) saw this Tony split ess and burst into flame. Capt. DRIER then made a direct astern pass on a Tony and it burst into flames near the wingroots and glided into the bay. Pulling up, Captain DRIER made another diving head-on pass at another Tony, who rolled, with Captain DRIER rolling with him, fell out of his roll, and disappeared into the clouds with smoke and flame pouring out of him. I was out of ammo, and Captain DRIER and I returned to base.

Capt. Joel B. Paris claimed his first victory in the P-38 when he downed a twin-engine ki-45 Nick ten miles outside Cebu City on Dec. 7, 1944. His fifth P-38 victory was a Zero over Clark Field on Jan. 1, 1945. He also had three victories with the P-40 in the 7th Fighter Squadron (one Oscar over Wewak on March 13, 1944 and two more over Biak on May 7, 1944).

Capt. "Ash" Aschenbrener, quiet-spoken ace from Wisconsin, was whisked back to duty in P-38s after he had already completed a tour in P-40s. He scored his fifth P-38 victory on Nov. 28, 1944 over Ormoc Bay when he claimed another Tony.   Aschenbrener

Fifth Air Force fighter battles reached a climax on December 7 when at least fifty Japanese aircraft were claimed around the Leyte area. Air victories for the V Fighter Command would never again exceed those proportions. Charles MacDonald claimed three fighters in the day-long action. Tom McGuire downed two in the hope of gaining on Dick Bong but the easy-going Bong also claimed two and frustrated the impatient McGuire. Meryl Smith had claimed two J2m Jack fighters before he failed to return from his last sortie.

The 49th Fighter Group had a good day, capped by Jerry Johnson's downing of three Oscars and a Ki-49 Helen bomber for the Group's 600th aerial victory. Johnson shouted over the radio for his wingman to watch three Oscars flying low over Ormoc Bay. Then, as quickly as he could count them, Johnson destroyed the three Oscars, leaving only three closely grouped oil slicks. Johnson later found the Helen bomber and sent it crashing into the jungle for his fourth victory of the day. Joel Paris started his string of victories for the 49th when he downed a ki-45 Nick over Cebu City.

Fernley Damstrom also scored for the 49th on December 7 when he shot a Zeke 52 down in flames. Damstrom's combat report gives some idea of the furious action around Ormoc Bay on the 7th:

. . . At approximately 1445 my wing man called in a bogie behind the convoy at 10 o'clock low, we were heading south at the time, to the right of the convoy at 7,000' or 8,000'. The ack-ack opened up and I saw the twin engined Nip plane as we made diving turns. There were other 38's below us and my second element had joined with Pinky Green. We went down to about 4,000' and I saw the Nip was heading for a destroyer which was turning out to sea. The Nip crossed the DD at low altitude and overshot but got a near miss with a bomb, several others dropping further on.

. . . At approximately 1455 a Nip plane sneaked in from the rear out of the weather and when I saw him he was at about 200' with A/A exploding all around him. When he was about a mile from a destroyer which was to the right of the rear of the convoy formation he started trailing smoke and headed straight for the DD which was again turning out to sea to evade the attack. It appeared to be the same one as had been attacked earlier. The Nip deliberately crashed into the destroyer and exploded half-way up the deck. The DD was smoking but still under power after the attack.

During two raids on Clark Field later in the month, Tom McGuire scored an impressive seven Zeros for his final tally of thirty-eight victories. On Christmas day, 1944, McGuire was leading fifteen P-38s during an escort of B-24s to Mabalacat Airdrome when about twenty A6m-5 Zeros jumped the Americans. McGuire looped his fighter and im-mediately exploded a Zero with a deflection shot. Within seconds, another Zero fell to McGuire's guns and crashed near the town of Mexico. McGuire was then under attack himself when he went to the aid of another P-38, but still managed to send a third Zero smoking into the ground near La Paz.

The next day McGuire was over Clark Field itself when a number of Japanese fighters attacked the B-24s. He closed to within 100 feet of a Zero and fired into the cockpit until the Japanese aircraft burned and exploded. In lightning-fast maneuvers, three more Zeros fell in flames, two of which were observed to crash in a dry stream bed. Thus, McGuire had secured a place only two victories short of Bong's record of forty. Only the fact that he had burned out his gun barrels in his furious attacks on December 25 had prevented him from scoring even higher.

It was just twelve days after McGuire had scored his final victories that the race of the aces came to a sudden end. In the latter months of 1944, in what amounted to a season of fallen P-38 aces, at least a dozen P-38 aces had been killed in accidents or combat. On January 7, 1945, the indomitable Tom McGuire was lost when he attempted to help a squadron mate who was being attacked by an Oscar over Negros Island.

McGuire was undoubtedly thinking of the safety of his fellow P-38 pilot when he pulled his fighter around in a tight, low-speed turn with external tanks still attached and fell off to crash into the jungle below. Other deaths were indeed just as tragic but somehow the loss of the seemingly immortal McGuire contained deep shock.

Air action subsided for the Southwest Pacific fighters during 1945. In effect, the air war for the Fifth Air Force had already been won. However, a few significant moments were left for the 49th Fighter Group. Jerry Johnson was fly-ing again with Jim Watkins, who had recently returned to the theater. Each pilot scored his final victory during a mis-sion to Hong Kong on April 2. Three Japanese fighters were racked up by the P-38 escort, of which Johnson and Watkins

L to R: George Walker, Bob Morrisey, Gerald Johnson, Milden Mathre, Wallace Jordan, Dick Bong, Tom McGuire, Bob DeHaven. Mathre scored the 49th Fighter Group's 500th air vic-tory on Oct. 29, 1944 and little more than a month later Gerald Johnson was given credit for the 600th victory.   Krane

Fred Champlin by his P-38L-5 "Eileen-Anne" with his final scoreboard.   Champlin

Dick Bong and Ernest Ambort at the 9th F.S. Headquarters in the Philippines. Ambort scored his first victory in the P-38 on Oct. 31, 1944, and was an ace by Christmas.
Ambort

Allen Hill when he took command of the 36th F.S. (Diagonal wing stripe was squadron marking.)
Hill

Back row: George Laven, Gerald Johnson, Clay Tice. *Front row:* Bob DeHaven, Wallace Jordan, James Watkins. The Australian flag symbol represented an Australian fighter that Johnson mistakenly shot down in late 1943. Johnson reportedly disappeared every time an Australian came into the 9th F.S. area. However, Johnson is supposed to have met his Australian victory, offered a bottle of American liquor and the two became good friends.
Laven

each claimed a Tojo.

It was on June 21 that Maj. George Laven capped the final victories for the 49th during a strike on Formosa. Setting off with Maj. J.R. Wilson as wingman, Laven found and bombed a chemical plant in a town on the southeast part of the island. With the plant buildings flattened or burning, the two pilots split up in search of other targets. Laven found an engine pulling twelve flatcars and bagged the lot with a neat strafing job.

A few miles inland, another large locomotive exploded under the major's guns and the train of eight cars was set afire. Cruising to the north, Laven was surprised to find an Emily flying boat careering along at about a 1,000 feet. Although the Emily was fast and heavily armed for a seaplane, Laven made quick work of the craft, watching it crash amidst some buildings along the shore. The victory happened to be the 49th's last of World War II, and, combined with his four tallies in the Aleutians, made Laven the war's last P-38 pilot to become an ace.

In all, the P-38s of the V Fighter Command had claimed 1,358 Japanese aircraft in the air. It is also fair to state that other fighter types in the command owed some of their victories to the ability of the P-38 to disperse and drive Japanese aircraft into their range. More P-38 aces were generated in the V Fighter Command than in any other organization.

Perhaps the value of the P-38 in the Southwest Pacific can be illustrated by an incident related at the end of the war by a veteran of the 8th Fighter Group. One day in 1945, cries of distress were heard over the radio somewhere above the China seas, "My engine's hit, I'm losing coolant; what'll I do!" Savvy P-38 pilots in the air at the time tried to advise the obviously green fellow in distress, "Calm down and feather it."

Then came the dejected reply, "feather, hell, I'm flying a P-51!"

MacDonald's "Putt-Putt Maru" after a taxiing accident in the Philippines.

Laven's P-38 in flight.   Laven

Captains Ken Hart, John Pietz and Lt. Horace Reeves scored some of the last victories and became the last aces of the 431st F.S., 475th F.G. On March 28, 1945, over Ben-Goi Bay on the Indo-Chinese mainland the 431st ran into a mixed group of Japanese fighters and Hart and Reeves claimed two Hamps each while "Rabbit" Pietz accounted for a Tojo.

"Duckbutt" Watkins and his ever-present pipe beside his P-38L-5 s/n 44-26407 "Charlcie Jeanne," named after his wife, after his April 2, 1945, victory over the Tojo.   Laven

Horace Reeves' P-38 "El Tornado" after he assumed command of the 431st F.S.

Chapter 5
China-Burma-India
"Twin-tailed Dragons"

*O*NLY TWO P-38 SQUADRONS FLEW ANY extensive operations in the CBI theater. The 449th Fighter Squadron was formed from planes and pilots who volunteered to fly in from the North African theater in July 1943. Organized and disbanded completely within the borders of Burma, the 459th Fighter Squadron was the only American unit formed outside the continental U.S. that never saw service within its parent country. It is only speculation what could have been accomplished if a complete group would have been formed but, as it is, nearly twenty percent of the theater aces were generated by the two squadrons. Japanese Army Air Force personnel who were interrogated after the war claimed that the P-38 was the most feared Allied aircraft in Burma.

The 449th Squadron was based at Ling-Ling and began operations around the beginning of August. Former Flying Tiger Maj. Ed Goss led the squadron on its first few missions and then future P-38 ace Capt. Sam Palmer took over. Palmer scored his first victory on August 26.

Lee Gregg was another 449th pilot who would become an ace with his P-38. Gregg had one victory scored with the 1st Fighter Group and began his 449th tally with a Zero on September 10. On an escort over Canton, Gregg and his wingman attacked what they thought were two lone Zeros hovering over the American dive-bombers below, but what appeared to be only two turned out to be sixteen. The pair of Americans headed right into the middle of them!

Fortunately for Gregg and his wingman, the Japanese were more occupied with the dive-bombers and ignored the two P-38s. Gregg selected one Zero that seemed somewhat separated from the rest and then attacked. The Zero turned out to be no novice and worked around to the tail of Gregg's wingman. Gregg tried to warn his comrade to break in the opposite direction but apparently one of the radios was not working. In the ensuing action, Gregg managed to claim the Zero shot down but his wingman received heavy damage. When he finally landed his damaged Lightning, all the control cables broke and the P-38 taxied with its control surfaces flapping and clattering like an angry hen.

That very few 449th P-38s were lost in aerial combat is probably due to the fact that enemy pilots were not keen on facing the strange new American fighter. The P-38 usually had an altitude advantage over the Zero and Japanese pilots learned quickly not to face the P-38s firepower in a head-on pass. This may be why the Japanese came over the 449th base only once in eight months, yet were attacking other American bases.

Perhaps the most desperate mission flown by the 449th was the raid against Kiukiang on October 30. Nine P-38s took off for the river-shipping strike but a bad omen loomed over the flight when Lieutenant Robinson was quickly forced to cut short the mission.

Over Kiukiang, the eight P-38s sighted twelve Japanese fighters waiting to jump them. Tom Harmon, the former Michigan football star, saw Bob Schultz lead two other P-38s into one formation of six fighters. Harmon pulled the release for his external tanks but couldn't be sure the tanks dropped. He disregarded the tank factor and turned into another flight of Japanese. One fighter came into his sights and Harmon fired, observing his target's canopy fly off and smoke pour from the engine.

But enemy planes seemed to be all around. Just as Harmon saw another fighter explode before his guns, cannon shells burst against the armor plate in his P-38 cockpit. One shell severed the primer handle between his legs and sent flaming gasoline pouring into the cockpit. Harmon tried to beat the fire out with his gloved hands but it was so intense that he had to leave his P-38, now in a near ninety-degree dive. Harmon had no idea how much altitude he had left so, when the canopy was released and the resulting suction ripped him out of the Lightning, he pulled the D-ring immediately.

As soon as his parachute opened, Harmon regretted his haste. There were still at least several hundred feet to fall and the two enemy fighters that had felled him were making lazy circles around his parachute. Feigning death seemed to be his only hope and Harmon sagged in the harness, hoping to outfox the curious Japanese.

Out of a corner of his eye, Harmon managed to see some of the ongoing battle. He was able to identify the P-38 flown by Bob Schultz and watched it tear head-on into two Tojos and bring them both down in a single pass. Schultz then roared at high speed out of the trap. Harmon also saw Lieutenant Robbins' P-38 going down, trailing smoke.

P-38G-10 "Golden Eagle," flown by Bob Schultz (who later changed his name to Shoals after the war). He flew this P-38 from Ireland to China. Shoals is still convinced that his bomber victory of November 1943 was a German JU-87. USAF

Relieved that the Japanese hadn't shot at him, Harmon landed in a lake and made for shore. It was a thirty-two day walk back to his own base.

When he returned, Harmon learned the full cost of that particular mission. Captain Enslen had been killed and three other P-38s had been lost. Lieutenant Robbins had escaped from the P-38 Harmon had seen shot down and Lieutenant Taylor had also escaped his broken P-38 to return to base. Half the flight had been wiped out for a claim of about four Japanese fighters, which was a virtual defeat considering that in this theater American aircraft were at a premium.

Some vengeance was taken while Harmon was walking back, however. On November 25, eight P-51s of the 23rd Fighter Group in company with eight P-38s of the 449th and fourteen B-25s crossed the Formosa Straits to attack Japanese airfields on Taiwan. Perfect surprise enabled the P-38s to claim twelve aerial victories. Captain Palmer chalked three more victories and Bob Schultz claimed a transport and a bomber. The day was made even better when all P-38s returned to Ling-Ling.

Squadron victories became rarer through the rest of the war even though Schultz and Gregg were aces before the summer of '44. One other pilot who is mentioned in squadron records is Lt. Keith Mahon, who outmaneuvered a ki-45 "Nick" for his first victory on February 10, 1944. He would score the squadron's last three air victories on January 5, 1945, and would total five air and five ground victories by the end of the war.

At the same time that the 449th was celebrating its Thanksgiving victory, the other operational P-38 squadron was just getting under way in Burma. Known as the "Twin-tailed Dragons," the 459th began operations on November 20, primarily as escort for bombers striking such targets as Rangoon and Meiktila. Initial operations were apparently uneventful for the young P-38 unit as few encounters were reported during the first escort operations. The Dragons made their own opportunities, however, and took a special interest in harassing Japanese aircraft over the enemy's own airfields.

459th F.S. emblem. Sophus Larson

Lt. Amal Boldman of the 459th in his P-38H-5 "Katy Did II" February 1944.   U.S. Army

Lt. A. Greco in P-38H-1 Miss'-ippi Hone'e' February 1944.   U.S. Army

459th F.S. P-38s about to take off on a bombing mission over India in February 1944.   U.S. Army

P-38J-10 of the 459th being serviced in the spring of 1944. IWM

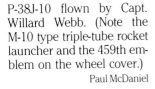

P-38J-10 flown by Capt. Willard Webb. (Note the M-10 type triple-tube rocket launcher and the 459th emblem on the wheel cover.)
Paul McDaniel

Operating from an airfield at Cox's Bazaar, the 459th made its first big impression at Anisakan early in the new year of 1944. On March 25, Lieutenant Boggs caught two fighters just as they were taking off from an enemy field and sent them crashing back to earth. Boggs had just destroyed another aircraft on the ground when he noticed a Zero going down in flames behind him as Lieutenant King shot the fighter off Boggs' tail. Bill Duke contributed to the destruction of two fighters during the encounter and his description of the air battle gives some indication of the Dragon spirit:

Over Anisakan, I spotted eight fighters to my right and a little below. I pulled up and went down on the first. I gave him a short burst and missed. I climbed again, got on another fighter and gave him a fairly long burst straight into his cockpit. I pulled up again and saw my wingman, Lt. J. Smith, shooting at him. He burst aflame and crashed into the ground. I saw another fighter below me and gave him a long burst. I saw my cannon shells strike true and the Jap burst into flames.

Several Japanese fighters were confirmed destroyed in the air as well as three others probably destroyed. Two Japanese aircraft were also claimed on the ground. The 459th losses totaled two P-38s.

Air combat for the 459th generally took on the same character in the months that followed as the squadron aggressively supplemented its required missions with sorties

Hampton Boggs' P-38.   Sophus Larson

Although his squadron records only credit Webb with about four victories, the Tenth Air Force gave him final confirmation for five, contradicting the usual major command practice of downgrading victory claims.

Japanese units had been suffering badly under the constant hammering of American strikes. The 459th, in conjunction with the P-51s of the 311th Fighter Group and aircraft of the 1st Air Commando Group, laid heavy destruction on Japanese aircraft, particularly the Ki. 43 "Oscar" aircraft of the 64th Sentai. On April 4, fifteen Oscars were burned on the ground by marauding P-38s and P-51s of the 459th and the 311th Fighter Group. Only two days after their successful raid on Heho, P-38s of the 459th claimed at least three Oscars of the 64th Sentai. The same day, Lt. Guichi Sumino, a Japanese ace who would eventually claim twenty-five aircraft, was wounded as he claimed a P-38.

A record was set by the 459th during the spring of 1944 with the 311th Fighter Group and 1st Air Commando Group. Two hundred and twenty-four Japanese aircraft were destroyed in the air and on the ground during the period March through May 1944. In its first fifty-eight combat missions of 1944, the 459th managed to claim fifty-six Japanese in the air and sixty-seven on the ground. The strength of Japanese fighter units was inexorably worn down; the fortunes of the Allies in Burma were conversely improving.

One exciting mission was flown by the 459th on June 6, 1944. The squadron divided into two groups to attack both Heho and Meiktila. Maj. Verl Luehring, the squadron commander, led one group of eleven aircraft and his executive officer, Capt. William Broadfoot, led the second group of seven aircraft. Captain Broadfoot, known informally as "B-foot," describes the action after both enemy fields had been attacked:

directly over Japanese bases. Another such mission took place on April 25, 1944, over the Japanese base at Heho. Early in the day, twelve Lightnings had paid Heho a visit and came home empty-handed. Later in the afternoon, however, the P-38s caught twelve fighters over the field and shot down six of them. The Lightnings then strafed the field, claiming two other aircraft on the ground, and returned without loss to their base. Capt. Willard Webb describes his combat:

> I attacked two fighters on the runway and black smoke simply volumed out. As I pulled up I saw three fighters in front of me. I chased one but he pulled away. So did the second. But I got on the third one all right. He was keeping on in a shallow climb, so I got in astern and opened fire at 200 yards. I saw lumps fall off his tail and fuselage and then the enemy aircraft exploded as it hit the deck. We left several fires burning on the airfield.

Major Luehring, first commander of the 459th, ca. November 1944.   Ethell

Capt. Walter "Bill" Duke, one of the top aces of the CBI.   via Ethell

At the western edge of the Burma Valley we were jumped from above by "many" Oscars and Zeros. We had some ammunition but not enough gas to fight. The total effort was to shake them off and go home. 1st Lt. Goodrich was shot down at this time. When he was finally clear and headed over the mountains, Capt. W. F. Duke radioed that he was missing his wingman, 2 Lt. W. G. Baumeister jr., that he had sufficient gas, he was going to make a circle back to make sure that Baumeister wasn't in trouble. Baumeister returned to base Ok but Duke didn't.

On that mission we compiled the following:

Major M. H. Glenn—destroyed 1 Oscar, capt. H. E. Boggs—destroyed one Oscar, Lt. R. E. Fertig—damaged 1 Oscar, Lt. O. R. Garland—damaged 1 Oscar, Capt. W. G. Broadfoot—damaged 3 Zeros, Lt. P. A. Jarvis—damaged 3 Oscars, Lt. I. F. Klumb—damaged 1 Oscar.

in a situation like this, some of the damaged were probably destroyed but, when you're trying to shoot your way out of a box, you don't mess around looking for confirmeds.

Whether or not they were confirmed, some of the actions of the day had significance for the 459th. Lieutenant Sumino, who had recently returned to action with the 64th Sentai, was in one of the Oscars that attacked the 459th that day. While he was on the tail of another P-38, Sumino was intercepted by one of the 459th pilots who sent a burst into the Japanese ace's cockpit, sending him crashing into the valley below.

After the war, Hampton Boggs was sent on an intelligence hop to various Japanese bases with the aid of an interpreter. Boggs discovered that when Bill Duke had gone back to look for his wingman he had been jumped by a flight of Zeros that was waiting for just such an opportunity. Duke had surprised the Japanese pilots by turning into them and downing three Zeros before he went down to his death.

One 459th pilot who might require special mention is Lt. Aaron Bearden. Somehow Bearden acquired the reputation of being a real dud and was ostracized by some of the other pilots of the squadron. Captain B-foot decided to put Bearden on his wing and find out what he was really like.

Lt. Aaron Bearden in the cockpit of his P-38.   via Ethell

-56-

Hampton Boggs, third commander of the 459th Fighter Squadron.   McDaniel

field. One Japanese aircraft was destroyed and seven damaged during the run but more than a dozen Oscars jumped the P-38s after the strafing pass was completed. Reacting quickly, both flights of 449th fighters turned into the Japanese attack. Mahon downed all three of the Oscars claimed by his flight and Wire downed the two claimed by his. Three P-38s were shot down but all pilots eventually returned.

It happened that both Wire and Mahon became P-38 aces during this mission. They had in fact become the last P-38 pilots in the CBI to achieve that distinction. Wire and Mahon were in the air again on February 2, 1945, practicing dogfights with their P-38s, when Wire's fighter developed some mechanical trouble and he bailed out, injuring himself in the process. His command of the 449th was cut short and he was sent home.

The final victory for P-38 pilots in the CBI theater came when Hampton Boggs found a Jill wandering the skies over Burma on a clear day on February 11, 1945, and sent it to earth for his final victory, according to 459th records. Boggs was the officer who interrogated Japanese air officers after the war and learned from them that the P-38 was the most feared Allied fighter in Burma. Whether or not those Japanese officers merely wanted to assure Boggs' good graces is unimportant. The fact is that the P-38 in the hands of CBI pilots caused the Japanese a good deal of anguish.

B-foot came to the conclusion that Bearden was as brave and dedicated a pilot as he had ever known and Bearden proved his leader's confidence by downing at least five Japanese aircraft in air combat.

Bearden was shot down on September 3, 1944, and captured by the Japanese. He ran into difficulties after the war when military authorities tried to court-martial him for allegedly helping the Japanese erect a captured, dismantled P-38. The charges were dropped but it is easy to see why he should be reticent about his military days. He was a brave and loyal airman who was treated unfairly.

When the Myitkyina area fell in the autumn of 1944 the Burma campaign was virtually over. No single factor accounts for its fall, of course, but the eager and tenacious spirit of the P-38 pilots should be given a share of honor. Their aggressiveness and courage made the formidable Japanese aerial presence less effective than it could have been.

Capt. Ralph L. Wire took command of the 449th at the end of December 1944. Wire had been credited with three Zeros over New Guinea during a previous tour with the 9th Fighter Squadron and he would fly an auspicious mission on the same day that Keith Mahon would score his last three victories.

On January 5, 1945, nine P-38s of the 449th and twelve P-51s of the 51st Fighter Group took off for a strafing mission on Hainan Island. The P-51s covered the Lightnings while they dived from 20,000 feet to the deck at Samah Bay Air-

Ralph Wire became commander of the 449th Sq. late in the war.

"Lighthorse" Harry H. Sealy in the cockpit of his P-38.
W. Broadfoot

Maj. Maxwell H. Glenn back in the U.S. on March 5, 1945. Glenn was possibly the victor over Sumino on June 6, 1944.   UPI

Two P-38Ls of the 459th Fighter Squadron.   via Ethell

Flight of four 459th P-38s on a low pass.   IWM

Chapter Six
Thirteenth Air Force
Lightning in the Solomons

*A*S THE 39TH FIGHTER SQUADRON worked up to operations with the P-38, things got grimmer on the embattled island of Guadalcanal. During November 1942, word was sent out for eight volunteers to reinforce the badly depleted defenses of the island. Bob Faurot led seven other volunteers of the 39th on November 14 with a B-17 for navigational escort. Future 39th Squadron aces Charles King, Ken Sparks and John Lane were among those who made the trip.

One of Charles King's first impressions when the flight approached Guadalcanal was pure wonder—American forces controlled no more than a 4,000-yard perimeter around Henderson field. In point of fact, the Japanese were among the first to greet the P-38 pilots when they landed—with an artillery barrage. Over the next few days, the 39th pilots shared the privations of the Americans on Guadalcanal including the bombardments and shelling.

There were several occasions during their stay when the V Fighter Command pilots shared alerts and scrambles on Henderson Field. King remembers one escort mission on November 18 that left him frustrated. His flight had failed to rendezvous with B-26s scheduled to attack Bougainville and missed sixteen A6m-2N "Rufe" floatplanes that tried to intercept the bombers. Further dejection fell on the 39th pilots when they learned that P-38s of the 339th Fighter Squadron had fended off Japanese attacks on a B-17 formation and had claimed two fighters. If these claims were indeed confirmed they would be the first P-38 victories in the South Pacific.

Conditions improved on Guadalcanal and the 39th crews returned to New Guinea by November 22. They left behind some potentially devastating comrades-in-arms. The leader of the 339th Squadron was Capt. John Mitchell who had been having some success with the P-39 Airacobras of the 67th Fighter Squadron. He wanted to instill some fighting spirit in the pilots of the squadron who had decided that the Airacobra was no match for the Japanese.

Mitchell led the way for the squadron, claiming a Japanese raider on October 9 and then another on October 23, 1942. He and Robert Ferguson each got another Japanese aircraft on November 7 and then he was given command of the newly arrived 339th Fighter Squadron and its

P-38s. Mitchell rubbed his hands in anticipation of the Lightning's potential. Besby Holmes, Douglas Canning and he greeted pilots like Tom Lanphier and Rex Barber who would share some significant actions in the coming months.

Mitchell got his first confirmed victory in the Lightning on January 5 and Besby Holmes scored for the first time in the same battle. Tom Lanphier scored several probables and confirmed victories during the end of 1942 and beginning of 1943. He claimed a Zero on December 24 and another on December 26. Several other probables were credited to him before he was given confirmed credit for three Zeros on April 7, 1943.

On that day a swarm of Japanese dive-bombers covered by Zeros was intercepted by the 339th. Lacing into the Japanese formation, the P-38 squadron downed at least seven Zeros, including Lanphier's three and two others for Rex Barber. Barber had claimed one other Japanese on December 28.

John Mitchell continued to score against the Japanese and became an ace on January 27, 1943, when he flamed two Zeros. He made a spectacular victory on the night of January 29 when he took a radar-equipped P-38 up to intercept a marauding twin-engine bomber. Lights dazzled the darkened sky over Guadalcanal when Mitchell's tracers burned a true course to the Japanese bomber's fuel tank and exploded the Betty with a brilliant flash. On February 27, Mitchell became a P-38 ace when he destroyed yet another Zero during an escort of B-17s. Besby Holmes claimed his fourth Zero in the same battle.

The American victories over Guadalcanal were more than ordinary in that the cream of Japanese naval pilots were involved in the counteroffensive over the area. The famed Tainan Air Corps, which had enjoyed unremitting success over the Philippines and the Dutch East Indies and lately over New Guinea, was operating its Zeros in a determined effort to retake Guadalcanal. Lt. Hiroyoshi Nishizawa and Lt. Tetsuzo Iwamoto were active during the period and each was reputed to have shot down more than fifty American aircraft in the Solomons campaign.

Thus, it was not always an assured victory for American pilots in the area. One particularly costly day came on February 14, 1943, when a mixed formation of Army and

Marine fighters was jumped by Zeros. Two F4U Corsairs, two P-40s and the entire top cover of four P-38s were shot down. It was one of the most costly missions that the P-38s flew during the Pacific war. Only one Zero was claimed by the Lightnings.

But the lessons were learned and the pilots of XIII Fighter Command, which came into being on January 13, 1943, developed a confidence that did not fail them. That confidence was sorely tried when the rugged veterans of the 339th Fighter Squadron were called on to fly the most famous P-38 mission of World War II.

On April 18, 1943, the 339th Squadron undertook its classic long-range interception mission. Four days previously, the word had reached the Navy Department that Adm. Isoroku Yamamoto, commander of the Imperial Japanese Fleet, would be traveling in the Kahili area on April 18. "Dillinger" was the ominous code word that was chosen for the Japanese admiral and eighteen P-38s of the 339th were selected to be led by Mitchell to intercept Yamamoto some 400 miles from Guadalcanal.

The P-38 was the only fighter aircraft available that was able to make the long-range run. Special 310-gallon external tanks were flown in to facilitate the range requirements of the P-38 and, although the operation was supposed to be highly secret, many of the Navy and Marine personnel on Guadalcanal offered help with navigation and targeting problems.

Eighteen Lightnings took off at about 7:30 a.m. on April 18. Two P-38s quickly aborted but the remaining sixteen successfully followed their circuitous route at low altitude. The tropical sun was brutal against the plexiglass canopies as the plane flew at minimum height and the external tanks under the wings of the Lightnings had no baffles installed.

Douglas Canning being congratulated for his part in the Yamamoto mission. Canning broke radio silence to call out Yamamoto's bombers.　　　　　　　USAF

Besby Holmes being congratulated by Gen. Strother after the Yamamoto mission.　　　　USAF

Gen. Dean Strother pins the DFC and Silver Star on Tom Lanphier after the Yamamoto mission.   USAF

As a result, every movement caused fuel to slosh freely, throwing the aircraft out of trim.

Lt. Doug Canning broke the radio silence at a few minutes before 10 a.m. when he called in enemy aircraft above the P-38 formation; two Mitsubishi Betty bombers were about to land with an escort of six Zeros. Lanphier and Barber quickly broke for one bomber and Holmes turned for the other with Lt. Ray Hine on his wing.

Barber and Lanphier were still a few miles from the bomber in which Yamamoto was flying when they saw the drop tanks fall from the three Zeros on their side of the Betty. They knew the Japanese were alerted. Lanphier zoomed head-on into the trio of Japanese fighters and fought a brief duel with the leader. They were still several hundred yards apart when their tracers crossed and, as the Zero passed him, Lanphier looked around and was sure that the Japanese had lost a wing and spun into the ground.

Lanphier was able to see in one brilliant second the Zero crash; the other two fighters overshoot both Lanphier and Barber, who was behind him engaging other Zeros. With the way now clear, Lanphier dived headlong for Yamamoto's plane, now almost invisible with its green camouflage as it skimmed the roof of the jungle.

Lanphier described the subsequent attack:

I realized on the way down that I had picked up too much speed, that I might overshoot him. I cut back on my throttles. I crossed my controls and went into a skid to brake my dive.

The two Zeros that had overshot me showed up again, diving toward Yamamoto's bomber from an angle slightly off to my right. They meant to get me before I got the bomber. It looked from where I sat as if the bomber, the Zeros and I might all get to the same place at the same time.

We very nearly did. The next three or four seconds spelled life or death. I remember suddenly getting very stubborn about making the most of the one good shot I had coming up. I fired a long steady burst across the bomber's course of flight from approximately right angles.

The bomber's right engine, then its right wing, burst into flame. I had accomplished my part of the mission. Once afire, no Japanese plane stopped burning, short of blowing up. The men aboard the bomber were too close to the ground to jump.

Barber also claimed one of the Zeros shot down and freed himself from interference by the escort to attack the other bomber. Vice Admiral Matome Ugaki was aboard that Betty and was at first puzzled by the bomber pilot's maneuvering just before landing. Ugaki was horrified when he looked out the window and saw Yamamoto's bomber trail bright flames and crash into the jungle.

In a moment, Ugaki also saw the unmistakable shape of a P-38 with its nose wrapped in flame as it made firing passes at his own Betty. With curious detachment, the admiral marvelled at the excellent gunnery of the enemy pilot whose bullets tore the Betty apart and killed most of the crew. The pilot of the bomber did the only thing he could and dived the smoking wreck into the sea. Ugaki survived and was picked up badly injured sometime later.

By the time the battle was over, three Zeros had been claimed in addition to the two bombers. One of the surviving Zero escort pilots was recently interviewed and stated his belief that all Zero pilots returned. There is no doubt, however, that the two bombers were lost with most of their inestimable personnel. Holmes' wingman, Ray Hine, was the only American casualty when he failed to return.

Holmes was late in getting back when he made an emergency fuel stop on the Sunshine Island airstrip. When he finally did land a heated discussion developed over another Zero and bomber that *he* claimed. It was finally agreed that the official credit would be distributed to the entire 339th Squadron.

Rex Barber has an unusually keen memory of the events of the day and his account corresponds with Japanese records. From Barber's vantage, he and Lanphier attacked the two bombers from the direction of the sea while the Bettys were over the jungle. Barber saw smoke coming from the right engine of the bomber he attacked and then it disappeared when it rolled sharply under his P-38. Barber saw what he believed to be the same Betty, still trailing smoke from its engine, out over the water with Holmes and Hine making a very fast pass from the rear. After a brief burst of fire, the two P-38s overshot the bomber and ran into several Zeros ahead.

Within the space of a few seconds, Barber saw Hine flying out to sea with smoke trailing behind his P-38 just before Barber slid behind the Betty and watched it blow up from his burst of fire. Barber's account seems to agree with Ugaki and perhaps gives the clearest light on the demise of one of Japan's most capable leaders. At least one Zero fell with the two bombers.

Nevertheless, Japanese attacks continued against the Solomons. Bill Harris, who was to become the leading P-38 ace of the Thirteenth Air Force, scored against two Zeros when a formation made a sweep down the Slot on June 7. He was in action again on June 16 when a big Japanese strike came at about 12:30 p.m. After sending two Zeros down in flames his four .50-caliber guns stopped firing. He attacked yet another Zero until his cannon ammunition was exhausted and he was forced to withdraw.

On the same day, Murray Shubin and his flight were about fifty miles west of Guadalcanal at 29,000 feet getting directions from Henderson Field radar when they spotted a formation of Vals and Zeros. The Americans were about 6,000 feet higher than the Japanese and had the advantage of the sun behind them when they spread out into battle formation and attacked the enemy.

Shubin wrote a letter shortly after the war describing the remarkable action that ensued:

[We] dove into the unsuspecting rear of the Nip formation, opening fire. Six flamers went down, only four were claimed.

Our attack broke up the Jap fighter cover, and we commenced combat. The dive bombers proceeded onward where they were met at the target by waiting P39s, P40s, and Navy fighters.

In the ensuing combat we got separated from each other. My wingman returned home with a shot-up engine and the other two returned after expending their ammunition.

I was left with six Zeros. I had already gotten two flamers, one on the initial attack and one immediately afterward as the Zeros pulled up in chandelles as a first reaction to the attack.

The six Zeros were evidently a group of very new and very stupid pilots because they never made any effort to break up in elements and attack me from different directions, but blindly followed their leader in a loose string, one behind the other. I was able to position myself by superior climb and speed at altitude to make attacks on the last one in the string. It took 45 minutes, but I managed to get four of them.

. . . The combat took place over the edge of Guadalcanal in full view of infantry troops and aviation personnel. Simultaneously, two other groups of Jap formations proceeded on to the shipping targets in the harbor. There they met the full fury of antiaircraft guns plus the eager and waiting P39s, P40s, Navy fighters and another flight of P38s. There were flamers going down everywhere—all Jap.

More P-38s were assigned to the XIII Fighter Command and by October the 44th Fighter Squadron was completely converted to the Lightning. Pilots like Coatsworth Head and Robert Westbrook had already become aces with the 44th in their P-40s. Westbrook had been in the theater since August 1942 and would be rated as one of the most skilled pilots to fly the P-38 in the XIII Fighter Command. He had scored seven victories in the P-40 and would claim at least thirteen

Lt. Col. Bob Westbrook by his P-38 in September 1944. Aircraft named "Florida Thrush." USAF

Westbrook probably during a break between opera-. tional tours. USAF

more in the P-38 to become the top-ranking ace of the Thirteenth Air Force.

Meanwhile, on October 4 Bill Harris had claimed his fifth Zero during an escort of B-24s over Kahili. Three days later he downed yet another Zero when the 339th again took the bombers to Kahili. The next day Harris received some notice for his impressive record when he was promoted to captain.

October 10 was the day when all the big guns of the Thirteenth Air Force P-38 squadrons went on another escort of B-24s to Kahili. Several Zeros tried to interfere with the bombing and lost at least three of their number to Harris and one each to Westbrook and Murray Shubin. Shubin is also credited with another Zero perhaps claimed on a separate mission, according to records of the time.

Bougainville Island was invaded by American Marines on October 27 and fighter cover was provided in part by Lightnings of the 339th Fighter Squadron. The Marines went ashore on Treasury Island in the first phase of the operation and the Japanese responded with an attack by Val dive-bombers. At about 3 p.m. eight P-38s of the 339th jumped the Japanese formation and claimed seven shot

down. Murray Shubin set fire to two bombers for his eleventh and final victory. Bill Harris got another of the bombers to score his tenth claim.

A few weeks after this mission Murray Shubin would be on his way home for good. He had a unique place among the P-38 aces of the Pacific. His five victories in a single combat on June 16, 1943, was never duplicated by another P-38 pilot in the theater. Nearly every top Lightning ace in the area was able to score four victories in a single combat but Shubin was the only man to claim five in a day. Shubin and his old friend from air cadet days, Eddie Gardner, were often seen flying together over Guadalcanal as happy as larks. They were an inseparable and potent combat team until Gardner was posted missing from a flight in July. Shubin himself was killed in an automobile accident in 1956.

The combat over the Solomons went on. On November 1, seven more Japanese aircraft fell to the guns of 339th P-38s, which were covering the Bougainville landings. Ben King downed a Zero for his third victory. He would later go to the European theater with other 339th pilots like Darrel Cramer and John McGinn and claim at least four German fighters with the P-47s of the 359th Fighter Group.

On November 11 the XIII Fighter Command P-38s began flying missions to Rabaul. From that date until the base was considered neutralized in March 1944 the P-38s would claim the majority of their scores in the Rabaul area. Ten Japanese aircraft were claimed by P-38s over Bougainville on November 8 and George Chandler and Thomas Walker claimed two definites each, raising each man's P-38 victory total to three.

Bob Westbrook had become the leading ace of the Thirteenth Air Force by the end of the year with some spectacular performances that earned him another Distinguished Flying Cross. On December 23 the P-38s were escorting B-24s over Rabaul when about twenty-five Zeros put in an appearance. Westbrook accounted for one of the Japanese fighters.

The next day Westbrook volunteered to lead another flight of 44th Squadron P-38s on a sweep over Rabaul. The Lightnings ran into eight Zeros and six of them fell to the squadron's attack. Westbrook claimed three. On Christmas day he volunteered to lead yet another sweep and sent two more Zeros down in flames. In the space of four days the master fighter pilot had flown four sweeps and had claimed five Zeros. He had fulfilled the most enthusiastic evaluation of his flying ability.

Westbrook's next victory came on January 6, 1944. He went home on leave sometime soon afterward, the top ace of the XIII Fighter Command with fifteen confirmed victories. But Westbrook was not through by any means and would complete seven tours of duty of various length.

Meanwhile, Bill Harris continued to score. On February 9 he claimed three Zeros on a sweep over the Admiralties and yet another pair of Japanese aircraft on

Murray Shubin standing by his P-38 before fifth Japanese flag was added.
USAF

Shubin watches as the fifth Japanese flag is painted on the nose of his P-38.
INP

Henry Meigs, George Chandler, Truman Barnes, Bill Harris and Thomas Walker—the 5 aces of the 339th F.S. in February 1944.
Chandler

George Chandler on "Barbara Ann IV." The other three P-38s named Barbara Ann were lost with other pilots.   Chandler

Col. Bill Harris in the cockpit of his P-38.
          Col. Harris

Left side of Bill Harris' P-38.
          Dwayne Tabatt

February 15. With fifteen victories to his credit he now stood even with Westbrook and went home on leave a short time later. By the middle of 1944 Westbrook was back as a lieutenant colonel at Headquarters, 347th Fighter Group. Harris returned about the same time, also as a lieutenant colonel, with the staff of the 18th Fighter Group.

At this time the entire XIII Fighter Command was equipped with P-38s; the only command in the Army Air Forces to be operated with a single type of aircraft. Preparations were made for the invasion of the Philippines and the XIII Fighter Command was based on Sansapor with the 347th Fighter Group on Middleburg Island by early September.

Westbrook was back in action and led the 347th with his example. He managed to down another Japanese on September 25 and downed his seventeenth victory on the 30th. He capped his remarkable scoring when he took part in a sweep over the Macassar area of Dutch East Indies by thirteen P-38s of the 339th Squadron on October 23. Six Japanese fighters fell to the 339th, including the three Westbrook caught over Boeloedowang airdrome.

Westbrook had flown on operations for more than two years and was certainly more than ready to end his combat days and return home. But, like other high-scoring aces, he was not willing to end combat while his talents could be used in air operations. On November 22, 1944, when he could have been safely on the way home, he climbed into his Lightning on the first mission of his eighth tour.

Westbrook and his wingman swept over the harbor at Macassar and spotted luggers churning a white lake in the water. The two P-38s went down for a strafing run and unfortunately ran into some accurate return fire. Both Lightnings were damaged and forced to make a fast break out of the area. But there was no escape for either plane; both made hard landings soon afterward. Westbrook's wingman was eventually rescued but the top-scoring ace of the Thirteenth Air Force went down with his Lightning.

Combat continued for the XIII Fighter Command but most of it was the routine escort and patrol variety. The combat fulfilled mission requirements but left little in the way of glory for the pilots, men who followed in the tradition of the Yamamoto victors and the high-scoring veterans of late 1943 and early 1944. Bill Harris put a fitting end to the record of Thirteenth Air Force aces when he downed his sixteenth Japanese aircraft during a sweep on June 22, 1945.

Capt. John Roehm's P-38 later in the war. Roehm avenged Capt. Cotesworth Head who was shot down on Jan. 18, 1944, when he led his flight into 20+ Zeros over Rabaul. Head claimed one Zero on Jan. 6, a Kate on the 14th and three Zeros on the 17th to become a P-38 ace. He also downed a Zero on the 18th before he was lost.   Roehm via Cook

Chapter 7
Eighth and Ninth Air Forces
Now is the winter of our discontent...

Big friend from little friend...
Big friend from little friend,
my fuel is up and I must return.

Little friend from big friend...
acknowledged. Thank you
for the company, little friend.

Big friend from little friend: good luck.

*S*O MAY HAVE PASSED THE POIGNANT
moment when the depleted fuel supply of the escort fighter forced it to abandon a stricken heavy bomber to the mercies of the cold and hostile skies of Axis Europe. When it was introduced to escort service in the spring of 1943, the P-47 was capable of an effective radius of action measuring no more than about 300 miles—or just inside the German border. When the P-51 was introduced into combat in December 1943, effective fighter cover was possible to any part of Germany. From January 1944 onward, after the range of the P-47 had been increased by some 100 miles, the Mustang and the Thunderbolt would be considered prevalent in establishing Allied aerial supremacy.

In the interim, however, between development of the P-47 as escort and the deployment of the P-51 to the European theater, was the brief period when the P-38 was committed to protecting the heavy bombers on the last leg of long range missions. On October 15, 1943, the 55th Fighter Group began operations with a sweep over the Dutch coast. Ironically, sixty Eighth Air Force bombers had been lost the day before, largely because of the absence of fighter escort.

First taste of victory came for the group on November 3 during an escort to Bremen. The 55th was given credit for three Bf 109s, Jack Jenkins claiming one Messerschmitt, and a young garage mechanic from southern California, Bob Buttke, claiming the other two. Just two days later, five more 109s were chalked up for the 55th's 38th Fighter Squadron when the Germans tried to set up a rocket attack on an American bomber formation but instead ran afoul of P-38 guns.

Strangely enough, these victories probably did more harm than good in that they fostered a sense of overconfidence in 55th leadership that would plague the unit throughout its tenure with the P-38. Group leaders would often commit the P-38 to battle at altitudes above 30,000 feet and seemed to ignore the hard lessons proffered to them by seasoned veterans who understood the wily enemy.

As it was, the 55th fought its first genuinely big air battle on November 13 when three Fw 190s, two Ju 88s, a Bf 109 and Me 210 were claimed. The cost, however, was prohibitive. Five P-38s were shot down by German interceptors and two others were lost to unknown causes. About sixteen other Lightnings returned with heavy battle damage. Lt. Gerald Brown, who was to become the 55th's first ace, came back with his aircraft ripped by hundreds of machine gun bullets and cannon shells. One engine was shot into scrap and a cannon shell plowed cleanly through a propeller blade.

Brown was in Joe Myers' flight during this battle. They were flying together about ten miles southwest of Bremen at 29,000 feet on a 210-degree heading after their flight had been split up by German attacks. However, the two P-38 pilots were able to maintain their protective charge over the bombers with dogged persistence, related by Myers' contact report:

We observed a Ju 88 approaching the middle box of bombers from the four o'clock position and at bomber level of 26,000 feet. We immediately initiated an attack upon him from above and behind. He observed our attack, fired his rockets and dove away to the right. I closed to within 500 yards, fired about a six second burst and observed his right engine smoking violently. We were losing altitude rapidly, so consequently I broke off the attack and pulled up into a spiralling zoom. As I did so, I observed an Me 109 on my wingman's tail about 50 yards behind him. I called him on the R/T, warning him and advised him to skid until I could position myself for an attack.

Lt. Brown took violent evasive action, doing dives, zooms, skids, rolls and various other maneuvers, but the German continued to follow about 50 yards behind, firing constantly. In the meantime, I moved to a position about 400 yards behind the Me 109 and using full throttle I was able to work up on his tail to a position about 150 yards behind him. I had already fired about three or four large deflection shots of about one or two second's duration at the German but without any noticeable results.

Finally Lt. Brown tried a skidding barrel roll, but the ME followed and put a long burst into Lt. Brown's right engine causing heavy brown smoke to pour out. At about the same time I had closed to within approximately 150 yards

P-38H of the 55th F.G. ready for takeoff, autumn 1943.

Penn

P-38H being guided by crewman, autumn 1943.

Penn

of the German and followed them both into the roll. As the German fired at Lt. Brown, I fired a five second burst at no deflection from an inverted position into the Me 109. His engine burst into flame and pieces of the plane flew all over the sky. I passed within 40 or 50 feet of him and observed fire from the engine streaming back over the fuselage.

Lt. Brown feathered his right engine and was able to make it to our home base.

November 29 saw another bad day for the 55th when another seven P-38s failed to return from a mission. When the cold and bitter northern European weather loomed ahead the pilots of the 55th shared the same bleak reality of the bomber crews who grimly considered the slender chances of completing an operational tour.

The painful truth of the November missions was finally brought home. German fighters, especially the Me 109, operated more efficiently at altitudes of 30,000 feet and higher. The P-38 performance suffered due to engine and supercharger vulnerability in the extreme cold. The P-38 cockpit also had no suitable heating for subzero temperatures and the control functions were awkwardly arranged. An Eighth Air Force tech report reputedly claimed that a major fault of the P-38 was that it was too complicated for inexperienced pilots. For example, manual release of the external tanks took five separate steps, a serious delay in light of combat conditions. Even so, the P-38 was valued highly in experienced hands.

Sadly enough, a type of pilot emerged, known as the "boarder," who went along on a mission just far enough to get credit for combat time. The bitterness of the hard-working ground crews also grew as a P-38, which they knew was in top-running order, would return early. Crew chiefs would slam tool boxes in disgust, knowing that their effort in the war was wasted.

But most pilots of the 55th were remarkably tenacious and fought on into the dark close of 1943 in spite of losses. On December 13, Bob Buttke's flight returned early from its escort duties to Kiel after one of the P-38s developed engine trouble. They were at about 25,000 feet around forty-five miles from Hamburg and twenty miles behind the bombers when they sighted Ju 88s. The Germans were called into the group leader and Buttke's flight went on its way.

Within a few minutes another trio of Ju 88s were observed and this time Buttke's Whiteman Yellow flight intervened. His report for the day describes the engagement:

Lt. Hoeper turned into the lower two going for the deck, while Lt. Hiner, Lt. Fair (No. 4) and I went for the one above. The two of us had from 10 to 30 degree deflection shot at him from slightly below. I was on the right and had less deflection from Lt. Hiner. I opened fire at about 350 yards and about three radii lead and let him fly through it. Lt. Hiner and I must have fired about the same time as there were strikes from one engine and wing into the fuselage, and from the trailing edge of the wing to the nose. The engine and wing caught fire immediately with pieces flying off in all directions. We swung around for a stern shot as he went by, but there was no need for it as the plane was burning and spinning fiercely with pieces still falling off. I saw one man bail out of the nose; his chute opened and we circled him once before starting for home.

Bob Buttke of the 343rd F.S. escorted B-17s to Brunswick on Feb. 10, 1944, and claimed two Bf 110s, then came home on one engine. P-38H-5 s/n 42-67047.   IWM

By the end of December another P-38 unit, the 20th Fighter Group, began operating with the Eighth Air Force. While the 55th was having mixed fortunes with the P-38 the 20th entered combat with enthusiasm. The best day that the P-38 had so far in the skies over northwestern Europe came on January 29 when three Fw190s, three Bf 110s, three Me 210s and a Bf 109 fell to the 20th Fighter Group. Capt. Lindol Graham made the most impressive show of the day when he claimed all three of the Fw190s with an average of only twelve cannon shells spent per victory.

The 55th was still facing difficult times but victories did come, evinced by Jerry Brown's report for January 31, a day when the group was flying escort for dive-bombers near Venlo and was bounced by about twenty Bf 109s from above:

My flight, led by Captain Myers, climbed to 33,000 feet trying to get above, and although we were holding our own, we could not get above owing to their initial advantage in altitude. Because of this we broke off and started down to rejoin the rest of the squadron. The enemy half-rolled and came after us. My wingman, Lt. Patterson, was bounced and I called for him to break left. The enemy aircraft followed him and got strikes on his right wing. Calling Capt. Myers to cover me, I broke down and got on the tail of the '109. My first burst from 100 yards at 28,000 feet hit him on the right side of the canopy . . . [I] closed to 50 yards and observed strikes all over his plane. His empennage blew off, as did his right wing tip. . .

Another squadron of the 55th was having a rough time in the same battle with some Fw190s. Capt. Morris Leve was shot down in flames. Lt. LeRoy Hokinson attempted to come to Leve's aid and shot down two Focke Wulfs in the unsuccessful try. Then a 190 heavily damaged Hokinson's P-38, setting fire to an engine and the cockpit. The 190 mercifully pulled off to one side to allow the P-38 pilot an escape opportunity. Hokinson had to rip himself free but managed to parachute into the hands of the Dutch underground and returned to England some months later.

If the Lightning was meeting with some derision from groups operating other types of aircraft, an incident early in February silenced at least some criticism. Lt. James Morris had only one victory, shared with two other pilots, until the morning of February 8. On that day he set an unofficial Eighth Air Force record by downing four German fighters in one combat. He described the victories in his combat report:

. . . As Col. Montgomery pulled up in firing position he could not fire due to frosted windshield. He pulled away and I slid into dead astern of A/C and gave a two second burst from about 100 yards. Saw strikes and large piece of A/C fell off. Plane cocked up and started down as pilot bailed out . . .

. . . in vicinity of Sedan saw two FW-190s carrying belly tanks, which had just taken off from airdrome below. Leader called me and said: "Let's get 'em." I made a sharp turn to left dropping maneuvering flaps to aid in turning.

They turned toward us and Col. Montgomery and I made a head on pass at them. I fired very short burst at 400 yards as we went by. Immediately dropped flaps on passing and racked it in to left and came down on one 190's tail. Fired one second burst from 150 yards at 30 [degree] deflection and slid in dead astern at 100 yards firing another short burst. Saw strikes on E/A as he went out of control. . . .

. . . Immediately saw second E/A approximately 90 [degrees] from course so maneuvered in behind him. Fired short burst at 50 [degrees] at 75 yards, as he made sharp pull up into overcast. Followed E/A into rain cloud, fired another short burst from dead astern at about 50 yards in turn past vertical. Saw E/A go out of control and followed it out of overcast to regain bearing. E/A was spinning at 400 feet.

I tried to find flight but could not see any A/C and as light AA was intense in this area, immediately took up safe course home. Flew for about 10 minutes in clouds at 2,800 feet to avoid AA which was firing at interval over inhabited areas. In vicinity of Denain saw Me-109 ahead flying at 45 [degrees] toward me. Not wishing to give him the advantage of trailing me I made a 90 [degree] turn into him, closing dead astern as he made sharp pull up at which time I fired a two second burst from 200 yards. Saw crosses on Me-109 which was silvery color. Saw strikes near canopy and airplane went into falling leaf. This was at approximately 2,500 feet. I made a sharp turn to head out toward coast and looking back saw the E/A within 300 feet of small village still in falling leaf. . . .

Three days later, on an escort near Bonn, Morris and Lt. Ben Rader went to the rescue of 77th Squadron Yellow flight, which had been jumped by four Me 109s. Morris attacked a 109, which quickly rolled over and dived into cloud cover. Another Messerschmitt was persistently attacking a P-38 and, as Morris fired, the black-crossed fighter was badly hit, emitting heavy smoke and flame, finally spinning wildly into the clouds. Rader also scored on a 109 from which the pilot jumped. With this victory confirmed, Jim Morris became the first P-38 air ace in the Eighth Air Force.

While the battles of late 1943 and early 1944 had left their bitter mark on the two P-38 groups there were some obvious notes of optimism. Jerry Brown and Joe Myers had dueled with the deadly single-engined Luftwaffe fighters at altitudes considered prohibitive for P-38 operations. During November 1943 the 55th had lost seventeen P-38s on operations but claimed twenty-three German aircraft while defending American bomber formations.

But the disadvantages of the P-38 in northwest European operations became evident. The roll rate of the Lightning was not sufficient to follow German fighters in evasive maneuvers at high altitude and the twin vapor trails left by P-38s at higher levels were a distinctive mark that usually allowed Luftwaffe fighters the option to stalk or evade. Added to its other problems was the fact that the P-38 was still feared and misunderstood by many of the people who were responsible for implementing its operation in the Eighth Air Force. For example, operational training units were instruct-

Lt. James M. Morris on Feb. 20, 1944, by Col. Russell's "Black Barney."   UPI

Morris and crew chief by Russell's "Black Barney."   IWM

ing new P-38 pilots that the aircraft could not be operated above 30,000 feet, could not be put into a high-altitude dive and could not be maneuvered on one engine. These restrictions were not entirely true, but had a certain dampening effect on the fighting spirit of new pilots.

All the problems faced by the P-38 units were reflected in their victory totals later in February and early March. During the last week of February the Operation POINTBLANK missions were flown in a direct assault against the German aircraft industry. Of the more than 150 aerial claims by England-based U.S. fighters, P-38s claimed only 10. Again, during the first two great daylight operations over Berlin on March 6 and 8, of the 160 credited victories 12 fell to P-38s.

But some of those fell to a pilot who, with about eleven aerial victories, was unofficially acknowledged at one time to be the highest-scoring P-38 ace in the Eighth Air Force. Col. John H. Lowell had been a project officer on the P-38 program at Wright-Patterson Field and went with the P-38 equipped 364th Fighter Group when it moved to England in February 1944. Lowell claimed two Bf 109s over Berlin on March 6 and another pair of Messerschmitts on March 8 for a remarkable combat debut. He managed to down a Fw190 on April 9 to become, unofficially, the fourth P-38 ace of the Eighth Air Force.

Meanwhile, Col. Mark Hubbard had taken command of the 20th Fighter Group and determined that some fighting spirit should be instilled into the unit. Although he had no particular love for the P-38, Hubbard was an aggressive and resolute combat leader. Four enemy aircraft had been credited to his account before he took personal charge of the 77th Fighter Squadron on March 18. He flew hard against the Luftwaffe that day in an effort to present a personal example for the pilots of the group. He managed to shoot down two Bf 109s and shared another with his wingman, Lt. Alvin Clark. Hubbard was last seen on the tail of another German fighter, which was smoking heavily. Lt. Clark reported that he had seen Colonel Hubbard chase the '109 into the doorway of a church. The next anyone heard of Hubbard he was in the POW camp at Barth.

But the most tragic loss of the day took place near the town of Ulm. P-38s of the 79th Squadron had gone down to attack three Bf 110s that were in the process of taking off. Major Franklin and Captain Nichols each shot one of the German fighters back to earth. Capt. Lindol Graham and Lt. Arthur Heiden attacked the third aircraft. Lt. Heiden's combat report describes what happened next:

Red leader at 20,000 feet called in 2 Me 110s taking off from an airport. Red flight went down and when the E/A were 300 to 500 feet above the ground the flight was closing fast. One Me 110 broke to the left and Red Leader and Red 2 followed it. The E/A was travelling about 200 mph and Red leader about 400 mph and overshot after a long burst.

Lindol Graham during a light moment, sitting at desk.
via Cook

Red Leader made an effective pattern with combat flaps firing on each pass from 30 [degrees] and closing to dead astern. He made at least six passes in this manner firing from 30 [degrees] to dead astern and 300 yards to less than 100 yards. The E/A was indicating about 100 mph and Red Leader about 150 with combat flaps. On several passes Red 2 also fired from 300 yards and about 30 [degrees] and strikes were concentrated mainly on the right wing, wing root, right engine and right side of the fuselage. The E/A crash landed in the snow and Red Leader made a 360 and returned to strafe the plane. While strafing, he hit the ground, pulled up as if into a right hand barrel roll and while on his back his nose dropped and he crashed at about a 60 [degree] angle.

Graham had become an air ace in February when he downed two Me 110s. His last mission remains a puzzle when his record is taken into account. Lt. Heiden speculated in later years on the bizarre events that led to Graham's death. Heiden's reflective account only adds to the mystery:

What took place with Capt. Graham has always seemed strange and a bit of a nightmare to me. I was somewhat new to the organization and didn't know him too well but had gained considerable awe and respect for his ability and had felt it a great honor to be his wingman.

I sat back and covered him the best I could through several wild passes he made on the Me-110 but shortly he stopped firing and moved out to the left side. I did not, of course, try to analyze the situation but was impatient for my first opportunity to shoot at a German, so I barreled in at the 110 at full throttle. . . .

Heiden attacked the 110 and had to break away quickly when the rear gunner zeroed in on his P-38. He could see the tops of trees above him as he fought to get his aircraft out of the stall. When he was able to look around again, he was surprised to see Graham's P-38 creep up on the German so that the Lightning's propellers were just above the Messer-

TSgt Bill Morris, Crew chief on "Susie," P38J-5 s/n 42-67926, after Graham had scored his remarkable triple-kill over the three Fw 190s on Jan. 29, 1944. Graham used only 36 cannon shells to down the three German fighters.

Englehart via Cook

Capt. Lindol Graham and his crew by "Susie," late February-early March 1944.

Englehart via Cook

schmitt canopy. The German pilot quickly crash-landed his 110 into the deep snow. Whether he had some idea unknown to Heiden or was simply furious at the frustrating tactics of the German, Graham continued to react in a curious manner.

Heiden continues:

This whole thing was starting to get beyond my comprehension and what followed was even stranger, yet. We, Graham and I, circled around while two figures got out of the Me-110, stood for a moment, probably as surprised as I was, then Graham made a pass straight at them. Instead of going for cover of timber a short distance away, they headed out into the open, a deep snow covered area. They had gotten a hundred yards or so on foot when Graham came

in at them. I was directly behind Graham as he came down on the Germans. I saw them stop and turn, then Graham's P-38 blotted them from view. I felt Graham was too low but cannot say for sure. My impression was that his P-38's props were in the snow at about the spot the German crew had stopped but then he pulled up into a sharp Chandell type of maneuver to the right. As it traversed through 180 degrees, Graham's plane rolled on over, onto its back, the nose dropped and it crashed vertically from about 1000 feet. There was no apparent bailout attempt.

Why and what happened precisely I do not know. To me, this was a nightmare and I was in a state of shock. There had been no conversation on the R/T other than battles going on elsewhere. What would cause this type of behavior from a great pilot?

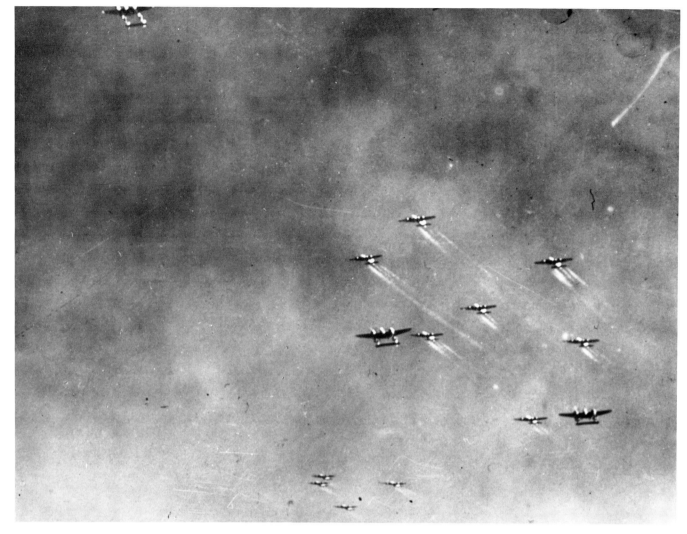

P-38s escorting B-17s over northern Europe.   USAF

Graham's loss was not the only agonizing event to plague P-38 units during the winter and spring of 1944. The units learned a painful lesson about unreliable power plants on May 8 when the 364th Fighter Group encountered a number of Luftwaffe fighters and some of the enemy tacked onto the tail of the group commander, Colonel Osborn. Capt. Roy Spradlin came to the colonel's rescue and shot down two of the attacking Germans and was firing at yet another when excessive manifold pressure caused one of his engines to explode. Spradlin parachuted into captivity. A few days later another pilot from Spradlin's squadron, Capt. John Ford, had similar trouble on takeoff and crashed to his death while he tried to land his P-38.

It was during this period that Colonel Lowell managed to raise the spirits of the 364th. An RAF officer had come to instruct the P-38 pilots in recognition of the Spitfire. The RAF pilot was also scheduled to demonstrate his new Griffon-engined Spitfire Mk XV in mock combat with a P-38. Colonel Lowell was urged by the pilots to fly against the Spitfire. He describes the contest:

Roy Osborn presenting John Lowell with a DFC. Lowell may have scored as many as eleven victories in the P-38 but faulty camera operation from the P-38's nose position denied many confirmations.   USAF

-73-

Gerald Brown in his P-38 cockpit sometime before April 1944. Brown destroyed a Fw 190 and He 111 on April 15, 1944, for his last aerial victories.   Gerald Brown

Operations Room, 79th Ftr. Sq., 20th F.G., Kingscliffe.
Jack Ilfrey

We took off and approached each other at 5,000 feet, so as to cross directly above our airfield. I was able to get on the Spitfire's tail, and he did everything in the book to get rid of me, unsuccessfully. In spite of the sharp turning radius and the high power of his new aircraft, I was able to stay on his tail in a tight Lufberry by flying what was known as the "Cloverleaf." I could not turn as tight as the Spitfire, but I could suck the nose of the P-38 in sharply, sufficient to get a good camera shot for a couple of seconds before the plane would be on the verge of a snaproll. Then I would have to release the wheel (stick) and push it forward quickly to prevent a stall which would move me to the outside of the Cloverleaf. After about 20 minutes of not being able to shake me the Spit pilot was obviously frustrated; so he took me over our own field at 1,000 feet above the ground and "Split-S'ed" to get rid of me. I followed him through with about a 30 degree angle off of vertical, and successfully stayed on his tail even though my P-38 came very close to the ground.

The Spit pilot was supposed to land and explain the excellence of his fighter craft to our group after the demonstration. However, he did not land, but returned to his base. That was the last we heard of him. Over 75 pilots witnessed that mock combat flight, and the morale of our organization was quite high.

Another demonstration, though hardly official, took place early in July over the home base of the 474th Fighter Group. Gen. Hoyt Vandenburg was present at a ceremony on the field when a number of 474th P-38s returned from a mission and buzzed the field, performing victory roll after illegal victory roll. An incensed commanding general demanded to see the offending pilots in his office, immediately! He intended to pin the tail on these donkeys personally.

However, when Vandenburg heard the stories presented by Lts. Huser, Banks and Milliken, punishment turned into award. Apparently, the general softened to stories like the young airman who persistently attacked a German aircraft in spite of a burned-out gunsight bulb and shot the enemy down with Kentucky windage. Milliken, as it happened, became an ace of the Ninth Air Force's 474th Fighter Group, the only fighter group in northwest Europe to retain the P-38 throughout World War II.

...Made Glorious Summer

Four additional P-38 groups became operational during the spring of '44. The last of these was the 479, becoming operational on May 26. A total of seven groups of P-38s constituted the maximum force for the Lightning in the theater.

Two days before the 479th started action, Jack Ilfrey, who

Ilfrey's P-38J-10 s/n 42-32843 with damage he received after ramming the Me 109.   Jack Ilfrey

was back in action with the 20th Fighter Group, found another hard time when he downed two Bf109s. Ilfrey had accidently rammed one of the German fighters and was last seen in a tight spin. Ralph Englehart, a member of Ilfrey's ground crew, remembers the events of that day:

Ilfrey was reported missing when the mission returned. We closed our tool boxes and were heading for the barracks feeling pretty low when a lone 38 came over. We could see it was MC-I and you could be sure there was a crowd and a lot of awe when we saw that wing.

Jack was very nervous, he always had his engine running before start time. He never waited his place in the taxi line to the runway but would leave the revetment in a blast of propwash and taxi so fast we were sure someday he would break a wheel strut on the curves as he actually rolled the tires so far the rims hit the pavement, but those P-38s were pretty well built. . . .

When he returned from a mission he would wheel into the revetment, set the brakes, cut the engines and be out of the cockpit standing on the wing before the props stopped turning or before any crewmen could get up on the wing. . . . The officers barracks orderly always claimed Jack had uniforms in his closet with 1st Lieutenant bars, Captain bars and Majors leaves as he made rank and was busted so often it was too much trouble to change bars.

Ilfrey also became a member of that elite club, evaders in enemy territory, after he was shot down by flak while strafing a train north of Angers on June 13. He simply dressed himself as a French peasant and walked or cycled toward Allied lines for four days. There was no lack of spirit in Jack Ilfrey.

Ilfrey by "Happy Jack's Go Buggy" after the final swastika had been painted on the P-38s side.   Jack Ilfrey

The jeep which Ilfrey commandeered for an English countryside excursion and which ended up in the Kings-Cliffe reservoir. Since Ilfrey was not authorized to take the Operations jeep off the base, he was heavily disciplined. The group commander interceded for Jack because he did not want a sub-lieutenant commanding one of his fighter squadrons!   Jack Ilfrey

The peasant dress that Jack borrowed to bicycle his way back to Allied lines after he was shot down on the June mission.   Jack Ilfrey

Although the decision to phase the P-38 out of Eighth Air Force service had already been made, there were some important, albeit token, victories scored by Lightnings of the northwest European front during the summer. On July 7 the 20th and 55th fighter groups accounted for twenty-five of the seventy-seven German aircraft claimed for the day. John Landers, one of the victorious pilots that day, was an irrepressible character who had claimed six Japanese in New Guinea before coming to the 55th Fighter Group. He downed one Fw190 on June 25, then ran wild on July 7, exploding three Me 410s in spite of some playful P-51s that made passes at his flight.

Jack Landers in the cockpit of his 55th Fighter Group P-38. It is not generally known that Landers scored half his victories against the Germans while he flew the P-38.
Don Penn

James Morris also scored his final victory when he attacked another Me 410. Unfortunately, the Messerschmitt gunner was accurate enough to shoot one of the P-38's engines and Morris was obliged to parachute into captivity. His final score with the P-38 was 7.33 victories, the highest official tally for a Lightning pilot in the Eighth Air Force.

The last P-38 ace of the Eighth Air Force began his scoring on August 14, 1944, during a freelance fighter rhubarb over France. Capt. Robin Olds of the 479th Fighter Group was on the deck and all alone in his P-38 when he noticed two Fw190s and managed to turn onto their tails (remember that Olds is *alone*). His report describes what happened to the undoubtedly surprised German fighters:

. . . Then I opened fire on the trailing E/A from dead astern, at about 400 yards, and fired a five to eight second burst. I observed many strikes on the left wing and the left side of the fuselage, so I changed point of aim slightly to the right and put a concentrated burst into the fuselage. I observed big pieces flying off the German aircraft and wisps of flame and heavy black smoke poured out from it. The E/A then went into an uncontrolled half roll going down to the right. At this time we were both just above the trees at an altitude of not over 100 feet.

The second E/A broke left in a violent evasive skid right on the deck and I followed, so I did not observe the first German hit the ground because my right wing blanketed him. I was turning inside the second German, so I fired in

short bursts at a range of approximately 350 to 200 yards, observing a few strikes. The E/A did a complete 360 degree turn and pulled out straight and level, still on the deck. Then I fired again, approximately a five second burst, from dead astern, and observed many strikes. Large pieces of the German ship flew off. He then zoomed and I followed, continuing to fire, still more strikes and pieces occurring. At the top of the zoom the German pilot parachuted, his chute opening almost at once, so that I had to cock up a wing to keep from hitting him. I saw this second German ship hit the ground and explode.

Brig. Gen. Robin Olds in 1968 while he was commandant of cadets at the Air Force Academy.   USAF

"Scrapiron" Larry Blumer being presented the Distinguished Service Cross by Gen. Carl A. Spaatz after the Aug. 25 mission.   USAF

Olds' audacity was matched by a Ninth Air Force P-38 ace a few days later on a banner day for the Lightning. August 25, 1944, saw the 367th and 474th fighter groups run into a mass of Bf 109s and Fw190s during a low-level sweep over central France. One squadron of the 367th was beset by Fw190s from veteran Luftwaffe unit J.G. 6 and was calling for help when P-38s of its sister squadron, the 393rd, responded. Capt. Lawrence Blumer, who was nicknamed "Scrapiron" because of the battered condition in which he brought back many of his aircraft from strafing missions, made the most of his part of the rescue and shot down a confirmed five Fw190s. Fifteen other claims were made by the 367th for the loss of eight P-38s. A Distinguished Unit Citation was awarded to the group for this action.

Twenty-one victories were racked up by the 474th but eleven P-38s were lost in the process. Lt. Lenton Kirkland tallied two '109s for the first of his five victories in the 474th.

Miles away, near Rostock, Robin Olds had just claimed his second Bf 109 of the day when he rolled over at high speed to help a P-51 that was being chased by another German fighter. Olds was stunned when his P-38 canopy ripped itself free as the plane was on the verge of a high-speed stall. Another German came in hot on Olds' tail but the cool P-38 pilot out-turned the '109 and sent it down in flames. Olds had become the first ace of the 479th and the last P-38 ace of the Eighth Air Force.

Gradual conversion to the P-51 began for the 479th about the middle of September when the 435th Squadron received a number of Mustangs. The P-38 had its last victory in the Eighth when two squadrons of the 479th downed about nineteen Germans southwest of Munster on September 26.

As it happened, a few victories were subsequently garnered by Ninth Air Force P-38s. Most Eighth Air Force P-38s were supplanted by P-51s in the period between July and September and most Ninth Air Force P-38s were replaced during February-March 1945. Only the 474th retained Lightnings until the end of the European war. One of the last moral victories was won for the Lightning on November 19, 1944, during an escort to Merzig, Germany. On that day a number of Fw190s attempted to interfere with a group of medium and light bombers and ran into P-38s of the 367th Fighter Group. Six Focke Wulfs fell to the Lightnings, including one for "Scrapiron" Blumer. No bombers were lost.

P-38J-25 s/n 44-23627 "Minnie II" of the 428th F.S., 474th F.G. at Euskirchen, Germany near the end of the war. Bob Hanson is at right.   Bob Hanson

364th Fighter Group P-38 undergoing repairs. Note the evidence of wheels-up landing, D-Day markings, locomotive victory markings and application of ball peen hammer mechanics.

Chapter 8
Twelfth Air Force from Torch to Salerno

...They were swifter than eagles, they were stronger than lions. —II Samuel 1:23b

*I*N THE FALL OF 1942 THE MEN OF THE 1ST and 14th fighter groups represented the best of the U.S. Army Air Force's fighter pilots. Highly skilled, professional and eager, they, along with pilots of a few other American fighter groups, would be the first to confront the Luftwaffe during Operation Torch in November. Flying en masse from England, the 1st and 14th were settled in their bases at Algeria by the middle of November.

Although they were not even sure that the base where they had been scheduled to land was in Allied hands, the two groups made the flight over the Bay of Biscay with only two men missing from the 1st Fighter Group. One of the missing men was Jack Ilfrey, who had developed fuel system problems and ran short of gasoline. He had to land in neutral Portugal.

Ilfrey was a young and impulsive Texan who quickly took exception to the Portuguese when they decided to intern him. But he readily demonstrated his P-38 to some curious armed guards. Ilfrey was quite familiar with the sudden acceleration of a taxiing Lightning. At the opportune moment he shoved the throttles forward and swept the guards off the wing with a sudden lurch. Losing no time in getting airborne, Ilfrey looked back and waved at his raging former hosts. Whether he knew it or not, Ilfrey had let himself in for some unique experiences in the months to come.

During their first few days in North Africa, the 1st and 14th quickly established a pattern of escort and ground support missions. The Luftwaffe was surprised by the initial appearance of the P-38 because their intelligence had not prepared them for anything like the Lockheed fighter—perhaps one of the rare occasions when a military secret was actually kept.

In any event, when veterans of the JG 27 and 77, equipped with the Bf 109G, first encountered the P-38, the Germans were astounded by its ability to leave them behind at full throttle. German pilots also learned quickly that bouncing the P-38 had special dangers since the initial zoom climb of the Lockheed fighter allowed it to follow the attacking Luftwaffe fighter racing for altitude and score a quick vic-

tory. Furthermore, it usually took the German pilots only one head-on attack to learn to respect the heavy, concentrated battery of four .50-caliber machine guns and 20-mm cannon in the nose of the P-38.

On the other side of the coin, Luftwaffe pilots considered the tactics employed by the early North African P-38 veterans to be generally ineffective. The big Lightnings would swing back and forth in great weaving arcs for mutual protection on patrols over enemy territory. German pilots thought that the maneuver made P-38 formations easy to divide and attack. The first contacts with the P-38 in North Africa also convinced Luftwaffe pilots of the Lockheed's propensity to catch fire easily. Dive limitations continued to hamper the P-38s' operations; enemy pilots could break off contact simply by making a split-s maneuver and diving away.

In contacts with Axis air transport, however, the range of the P-38 made it the prime interceptor of supply lines. On one mission of November 24 no fewer than sixteen enemy transports were destroyed or damaged in the air or on the ground by fighters of the 14th Fighter Group. Unit records of the period suggest that Lts. Virgil Lusk and James Butler were credited with at least four Savoia-Marchetti 81 transports each. Unhappily, it would be one of the last occasions

Jack Ilfrey in P-38F 41-7587 at Kirten-In-Lindsey, England, summer 1942. The same P-38 Ilfrey flew to England, made 22 missions then flew to Portugal, Gibraltar and finally Youks-Les-Bains in North Africa.

Jack Ilfrey

P-38 of the 1st F.G. at Biskra, North Africa on Dec. 31, 1942.　　U.S. Army

in which the 14th Fighter Group could rejoice during those days of the North African air war.

Several P-38 aces began their records on November 29, when both the 1st and 14th fighter groups were engaged in a strike against Gabes Airdrome. Jack Ilfrey had finished strafing Gabes and was leaving the area with Capt. Newell Roberts when he encountered two Me 110s:

> . . . . Captain Roberts pointed out two enemy planes (Me 110s). I shot bullets into both of them, and both planes crashed. Captain Roberts and I each claim 1/2 a plane apiece, and Captain Watson and Lt. V. Smith of the 14th Fighter Group who were in the flight each claim 1/2 of the other plane destroyed.

The pilot that Ilfrey referred to as V. Smith was actually Virgil Smith. Ilfrey and Smith share the distinction of being the first two P-38 aces of World War II. Unfortunately, since records for the period are sketchy and contradict with each other in some cases, there is no official documentation of the first pilot to become an ace. Ilfrey certainly claims his fifth victory with the downing of two Fw190s during an escort of B-17s to Bizerte on December 26. Documents suggest that Smith scored his fifth confirmed victory on December 28 but was tragically killed on December 30 when he tried to land his crippled P-38 in an open field and hit a ditch, exploding his fighter.

Earlier, Jack Ilfrey had nearly ended his combat career in a similar manner during a mission over Gabes on December 2. Once again Ilfrey's terse combat report tells the story:

> I took off at 0645 with Capt. Roberts, Lts. McWherter and Lovell on a fighter sweep. Our flight came on to the right of GABES Airdrome at about 0815 at 50 feet. We saw 4 Me 109s taking off in a string. I went after the second one

and gave several long bursts with both machine guns and cannon. His engine fell out and he did a nose dive into the ground, catching on fire.

The fourth Me 109 got on my tail at about 500 feet and gave me a short burst. I then got on his tail and chased him to south side of airdrome, giving him several long bursts with both machine guns and cannon. Pieces flew off and he crashed into a ditch. The plane was completely demolished and the pilot was lying half in and half out of what had been the cockpit.

At that point I climbed to about 1000 feet and dived on airdrome. There was 1 airplane on the ground with about 8 men around it trying to start. I gave it a very long burst with both machine gun and cannon and it burst into flame, the men around it falling away. Lt. Lovell had already hit this Plane.

Virgil Smith who is variously given credit for his fifth victory on Dec. 12 or Dec. 28, 1942. Since Ilfrey scored his fifth on Dec. 26, one of these two pilots is the first P-38 ace of World War II.　　USAF

-80-

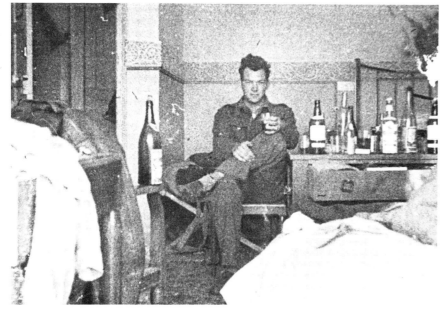

Ilfrey in the famous Hotel Trans-Atlantique described by war correspondent Ernie Pyle. Ilfrey is forcing himself to drink some "awful French stuff."

Ilfrey's crew chief battering for eggs at Biskra by Ilfrey's P-38.   Jack Ilfrey

Ilfrey by his P-38 in North Africa.   Jack Ilfrey

James Harmon, Norman Widen, Newell Roberts and Jack Ilfrey in England during the summer of '42. Harmon was killed in action, Widen was captured, Ilfrey and Roberts became aces.

What Ilfrey did not mention was that the Messerschmitt had damaged his P-38 so badly that he had to end the mission on one engine. Bill Lovell and Newell Roberts escorted him back to Youks.

December proved a bloody month in general for P-38s in North Africa. The 82nd Fighter Group joined the 1st and 14th at the end of the month to offer some relief from the arduous demands placed on the Lightning units. Escort for every type of bomber mission from B-17 to smaller B-26 and A-20 raids took its own toll on P-38 ranks.

The top aces of the North African campaign began their scores when the 82nd got up steam in January. Claude Kinsey of the 96th damaged his first Bf 109 on January 7.

He claimed another on January 29 and, during an escort to El Aouinet the next day, downed yet another plus a probable.

Kinsey was part of a sixteen-plane P-38 escort of eighteen B-25s on January 30 when the bombers passed up El Aouinet to bomb Gabes. During the withdrawal several Messerschmitt 109s attacked the bomber formation without result. Then, when the bombers were running for home on the deck, many Fw190s and 109s attacked. Six fighters were claimed by the P-38s, which lost three of their own number. Kinsey sent one Messerschmitt crashing in flames and and another trailing smoke.

Another pilot who scored on the 30th and was destined

P-38s and F-4s on line for engine run-up at Liverpool Airport, Speke, England on Jan. 16, 1943. By the end of January, all P-38s would be transferred to North Africa out of England.

to become the high-scoring ace of the theater was Lt. William "Dixie" Sloan. He destroyed one Messerschmitt on January 7 and outmaneuvered another during the January 30 show for his second victory. By the end of July he would be the top-scoring ace of the Twelfth Air Force. Kinsey would also become the ranking P-38 ace of the North African campaign with seven victories before he was downed and taken prisoner during the rout of German transports off Cape Bon on April 5, 1943.

Another real danger for P-38 pilots revealed itself during ground-attack missions. During an attack against German pillboxes that guarded a pass near Sfax, Jack Ilfrey again barely escaped with his life when German fighters jumped his flight. He flew home with one of his engines vibrating badly and the other shot out completely. Back at his base, Ilfrey counted 168 holes in his P-38 and eight cannon shell dents in the armor plate behind his head.

Most P-38 pilots in the North African war were not as fortunate as Ilfrey in similar circumstances. Capt. Darrell Welch of the 27th Fighter Squadron remembers that strict formation discipline was necessary for survival. He was leading Cagney White Flight during an escort of B-17s to Tripoli Aerodrome when one member of his flight decided to attack a German fighter and dived away from the P-38 formation to get his victory. Welch himself was then attacked by a Bf 109. His combat report takes up the action, which occurred at about 17,000 feet thirty to forty miles west of the target:

Darrell Welch's P-38 after April 5, 1943.   Darrell Welch

Darrell Welch's ground crew.   Darrell Welch

. . . . He [the Bf 109] came through the formation and I turned into him and gave him a long burst from his left rear quarter. He half rolled and I did not watch him as I saw a P-38 under with 2 Me 109s on his tail. I saw another P-38 chasing the 2 Me 109s and I joined the chase.

The 109s were slowly closing in. The other P-38 opened fire on the [rear] Me 109 from long range and he turned away to the left—apparently hit. The other e/a had closed in on the P-38 to close range. I was still out of range. The e/a gave the P-38 a short burst and I saw smoke coming from the P-38 which rolled over to the left.

The e/a pulled up into the sun and I followed, opening fire at long range. I was closing up still firing in several short bursts and I could see white smoke coming from him. He turned to the left slightly and half-rolled. I was too low to follow, about 4,000 feet, but I turned and dived at him. He was still out of range and my right engine cut out. I was forced to abandon the chase. I claim the first e/a as destroyed on Lt. SHAHAN'S statement and the second e/a as damaged.

The P-38 that had broken formation was shot down and the pilot, badly burned and bruised, was able to parachute into captivity. Welch remembers that he was repatriated only to die in another crash shortly after the war.

There were a great many losses during the escort missions flown by P-38s. However, those losses were suffered mainly by the Lightnings themselves. Forced to stay close to the bombers, the P-38 pilots would look in frustration at enemy fighters circling easily from their bases to superior altitudes.

On December 5, 1942, P-38s of the 14th Fighter Group were escorting twelve A-20s to Tunis. As soon as the bombers had completed their run, Bf 109s and Fw190s attacked from above. Later group estimates indicated that about sixty German fighters engaged the eight P-38s that comprised the 49th Fighter Squadron that day.

Bob Carlton, one of the few P-38 pilots to make it back, recalled the situation:

We were all split up, and it was every man for himself. The fight actually lasted around 10 or 15 minutes, but seemed like hours. We lost our C.O., Capt. Hal Lewis, his wingman, Lt. Elliot; and my wingman, a lieutenant whose name I cannot recall at this time. Lt. Gustke was shot down behind the lines, but showed up three days later. Lt. Earnhart was shot down on our side of the lines, but was O.K. Lt. Ribb, Lt. Working and [I] got back in one piece and all the A-20s returned unhurt.

The final score for this mission—five P-38s lost for

Pilots who scored 14 victories between them during one of the big routs of German transports on April 10, 1943, over the Mediterranean. L to R: Walt Rivers (4 confirmed), John Moutier (3 confirmed), Meldrum Sears (4 confirmed) and Lee Wiseman (3 confirmed and 2 unconfirmed). Pilots are from 71st F.S., 1st Fighter Group. USAF

three Germans claimed—became the typical story for many of the 14th Fighter Group's operations. Peril-fraught low-altitude support missions left the P-38s open to attack by enemy fighters as well as groundfire. Pressure was especially heavy on P-38 units because the P-38 was in demand for every possible type of mission, and thus frequently was forced to fly in small groups. The heavy attrition that naturally followed such commitment began to tell on the morale of the pilots. In the case of the 14th Fighter Group, the unrelenting pressure of combat would finally bring near-tragedy as the unit reached its breaking point sometime in January.

Lt. Col. Oliver B. Taylor was assistant chief of staff A-3 at the headquarters of the 1st Service Area Command (Prov) in Casablanca when he received a curious teletype message regarding the 14th Fighter Group sometime early in February. As well as he can recall, Taylor believes the message had four parts that included these items:

1. The 14th Fighter Group had disgraced itself in action.

2. Flying personnel and aircraft had been reassigned; the ground echelon was being sent to the rear pending their reassignment.

3. Accommodations would include the bare minimum in amenities at Casablanca.

4. The 14th Fighter Group would be stricken from the rolls.

Taking off in his AT-6, Taylor met the 14th Fighter Group for planning purposes at a field on its line of march. He was perplexed that what he saw did not fit the image suggested by that TWX. The 14th's ground personnel, Taylor discovered, were quite a cut above newer units in maturity and professional qualities. Back at his headquarters, Taylor implored the powers in charge with his conviction that disbandment would be a terrible waste and a grave injustice. Meanwhile, he made arrangements to move the 14th to the permanent French Air Force base at Mediouna. Taylor did this in open defiance of that part of the TWX about minimum amenities, certain that sanity would prevail and the 14th would be exonerated.

It was exonerated. The reorganization of the group commenced in short order under the command of Col. Troy Keith. A third squadron, the 37th, was added to create a full-strength group. What impact he may have had on the decision to absolve the 14th Taylor couldn't say, but when he got his chance at a combat command later in the year it just had to be the "Fighting Fourteenth." And so it was.

Meanwhile, the war pressed onward toward Tunisia. The 82nd continued its devastation of Axis air power into February when pilots like Bill Sloan and Tom "Ace" White claimed their fifth aerial victories. On February 15, 1943, Sloan claimed a '109 for his fifth tally and White claimed a

William J. "Dixie" Sloan on Aug. 9, 1943, after his score had been completed.   National Archives

Fw190 for his fourth. Two weeks later he shot down another Messerschmitt 109 to become an ace.

By the beginning of March the P-38 had become the dominant American fighter in the North African theater. Although losses for U.S. P-38s, P-40s and Spitfires had been high, the P-38 had claimed almost twice as many aerial victories as the other two fighters combined. The combination of its long-range and impressive performance put the Lightning in the forefront.

Back in the 1st Fighter Group, the P-38s record continued to be enhanced by pilots like Jack Ilfrey, a pilot who maintained his irrepressible ways in combat. One example that bears witness to Ilfrey's fortunes occurred when a Messerschmitt that he had been stalking maneuvered and dived into cloud to avoid Ilfrey's attack. Ilfrey quickly flew to the point where he reasoned the German would emerge. But Ilfrey was more accurate than he might have hoped —the German popped out of the cloud coming straight at him, only yards away. Both pilots happened to kick their rudders in the proper direction and missed each other by bare inches.

Another P-38 pilot who came into some prominence during the latter stages of the North African campaign was Lt. Lee Wiseman. Wiseman scored his first victory on February 4 when the 1st Fighter Group escorted B-17s to an attack on airdromes near Gabes. Wiseman's squadron encountered a mixed force of German fighters trying to intercept the bombers at about 22,000 feet altitude somewhere near the target:

> Our flight turned 360 degrees over a man in a parachute who had bailed out of a B-17, as enemy aircraft were making passes at him. A Me 109G made an attack on our flight from above and to the left. The flight leader turned into him and when I looked down to the right I saw a FW 190 with yellow nose, coming up to attack my wingman. I kicked hard left rudder and fired a burst from machine guns into him from 200 yards. He flipped on his side, belly towards me, and at 100 yards I fired another burst from machine guns into his mid section between the wings in the fuselage, noting that he started smoking all over and falling. At this time he was lost from my view and I rejoined the formation. Lt. George F. Prittin who was flying my wing, saw the FW 190 going down in flames.

In three big days of fighting off the coast of Cape Bon, Tunisia, about forty German transports and at least ten escorting fighters were shot down, mostly by P-38s of the 1st Fighter Group. Wiseman had his big opportunity during this period as he is variously credited with four or five Ju transports in a single combat. Walt Rivers is also given credit for four transports in one combat to make the two pilots high scorers for the series of interceptions on the 5th, 10th and 11th of April, 1943.

It was also during April that the 82nd Fighter Group began to establish its record as a crack fighter unit. Wartime reports give the 82nd credit for about sixty transports downed during the desperate Axis attempts to supply their armies in April. Things were not quite so simple against enemy single-engine fighters, however. One of the first of the 82nd's aces describes his first encounter with the deadly Me 109:

> On April 29, 1943, my third mission, we were on a skip-bombing hop over Cape Bon, and were attacked by twelve 109s of the famed Yellow Nose Squadron. We turned to fight and headed into a group of three 109s. After an exchange of shots, I turned and followed an Me. until he crashed. I then saw a P-38 on a single engine, being attacked by three 109s. I dove and caught them, getting two more. The third got away after shooting down the 38.
>
> Then I saw another single engine P-38 go in, and still another all alone heading for France. I caught up to him (Lt. Robert Wells) and escorted him back to Africa to the shore near Algiers, where we both were forced down for lack of gas. He crashed but came out alive. I landed safely, plane and all, in a river bed near Abbo, a little village 40 kilometers from Algiers. Engineers came down and laid 500 yards of steel mat, and I flew my P-38 back to base five days later. In the engagement we got seven Me. 109s and they destroyed three P-38s, and three came home on a single engine.

The pilot who flew this remarkable first combat against the Luftwaffe was Lt. Louis Curdes; he was awarded a Distinguished Flying Cross for the mission. It may be noticed that

Curdes claimed two of the German fighters while he was attempting to aid a stricken fellow P-38 pilot. Most of Curdes' victories were gained in a similar manner, which tended to make him a highly popular member of the 82nd.

By the beginning of May, the 14th Fighter Group had been re-manned and was operating against the Axis once again. Col. Troy Keith, who had been the original commander of the unit, was taking an aggressive hand in leading the 14th back into combat. One of the rising stars in the renewed 14th was Lt. Richard Campbell. Campbell had an auspicious debut in the victory column when he accounted for two Me 109s on a patrol over the Mediterranean Islands on May 18 and would score steadily during late spring and early summer of 1943.

Lt. Richard A. Campbell of the 14th Fighter Group had a reputation as a wild and fearless pilot. Once, when an enemy anti-aircraft battery shot down a comrade of Campbell's, he made several passes over the position and shot the offending gun into silence.   USAF

On July 5, five days before the Allies landed on Sicily, an air battle over the Catania-Gerbini area cost the Regia Aeronautica heavily at the hands of 82nd Fighter Group pilots. Flying Macchi Mc202 fighters, the enemy included Franco Lucchini and Leonardo Ferrulli with twenty-six and twenty-two victories respectively. Each pilot had been flying combat since 1940 and each had shot down several American fighters. Both Italian aces were probably claimed by 82nd pilots on July 5. William Sloan and Gerald Rounds claimed a victory each.

On July 18, three 14th Fighter Group aces had a day of good hunting. On patrol over the Straits of Messina, Lts. Paul Wilkins and Sidney Weatherford and Capt. Herbert Ross each caught and destroyed two Ju 52 transports. Claims for fifteen enemy aircraft were registered by the 14th on July 18 and just four days later "Dixie" Sloan scored two victories to culminate his bag of twelve. The patrols over the Mediterranean were indeed fruitful. Many of the Twelfth Air Force P-38 aces made their records during this period.

Aces of the 82nd scored many aerial victories in this part of the campaign. Frank Hurlbut became an ace on July 10, 1943, during a sweep over Sicily that netted the group ten victories. The top air ace of the Twelfth Air Force for keeps was William Sloan who had scored his twelve Axis aircraft by the end of August, when his tour ended. Flight Officer Frank Hurlbut followed Sloan with nine victories, scored mainly during the period before the invasion of Italy. Louis Curdes also made the last of his Mediterranean victories at this time. Two days after the 1st and 82nd fighter groups won Distinguished Unit Citations for a raid against grounded Axis aircraft at Foggia on August 25, Curdes was escorting B-26s over Benevento, Italy. When Me 109s jumped the American formation, Curdes once again came to the aid of a P-38 in trouble and downed two of the attacking Messerschmitts.

Curdes' bravery was not without cost on this mission, however. Four or five other German fighters were in the area and immediately jumped both American fighters. The other P-38, piloted by Flight Officer Melvin Sheets, was never seen again. Curdes had his own devil of a time escaping the guns of the Messerschmitts. Somehow he did lose his pursuers but not before many bullets and cannon shells penetrated his Lightning. Several shells exploded in the nose of his P-38, destroying his guns, and one of his engines was damaged. Trying to make his way back to Sicily, Curdes inadvertently flew over a flak battery at Naples. An accurate burst put out his good engine and by the time he reached the waters of the Mediterranean, Curdes decided his one ailing engine wouldn't make it. He landed on an Italian beach, set his aircraft afire and dejectedly waited for capture.

Another P-38 pilot was somewhat luckier than Curdes during a harrowing mission on August 21. Lt. Richard J. Lee of the 1st Fighter Group was escorting a bomber formation when his left engine began missing badly. Lee decided to trim his aircraft and continue the mission to provide additional firepower.

Over the target, about fifty enemy fighters were sighted making their usual climb to an advantageous height above the P-38s, which were still committed to stay close to the bombers. When the enemy began making determined attacks on the American formation, Lee turned his P-38 to face the interceptors in a head-on pass. With full power applied, the P-38's left engine suddenly exploded. Shaken by the disaster that threw his aircraft out of control in the face of heavy enemy opposition, Lee fought his P-38 in the dive and finally managed to master the careening Lightning.

A P-38 on one engine is difficult enough to manipulate. In a combat area buzzing with enemy aircraft, the pilot of a stricken P-38 should necessarily be discreet. But, apparently, Lee was too lathered and was certainly too good a fighter pilot to consider the better part of valor. Sighting a Macchi 202 or 205 attacking his flight leader from beneath, Lee cut inside the Italian's line of flight and sent him down in flames.

Six leading 82nd Fighter Group aces in the summer of 1943. Ward Kuentzel, Frank D. Hurlbut, Ray Crawford, Lawrence P. Liebers, William Sloan and Louis Curdes. Kuentzel was KIA with the 479th Fighter Group in 1944 and Liebers was killed in an aircraft accident after the war.   USAF

Lt. Richard J. Lee displaying the DFC he won for his first air victory on Aug. 21, 1943. (Medal on Lee's left is the Air Medal; DFC is on his right.)   R.J. Lee

Only then did prudence prevail and Lee scrambled for home. He was awarded the Distinguished Flying Cross for the mission. It was also his first victory.

Italy was invaded by the British on September 3 and the Salerno landings began on September 9. P-38s covered the landings effectively and countered most Luftwaffe reaction. Still operating from Tunisia, the P-38 groups also conducted long-range support strikes. It was on one of these missions that P-38 ace Donald Kienholz had just about the fright of his combat career. Flying over the Salerno area, Kienholz's P-38 was hit hard by a burst of flak and blown upside down. He was disoriented by the sudden change in flight attitude and all around him Kienholz could see intertwining laces of orange anti-aircraft fire. There was no time to consider corrective action, however, as another burst of fire hit his aircraft and righted it. He quickly took evasive action and set a safe course for home with one engine shot out.

Also in September, Col. Oliver Taylor and the 14th Fighter Group began a mutually satisfying relationship. Taylor had graduated from West Point in 1939 and won his wings in 1940. When he was finally given command of a combat unit, it was due to a certain effort on his part that the unit was the 14th Fighter Group. Col. Taylor first led the 14th on a dive-bombing strike on September 27.

During the autumn of 1943, Axis forces threatened British control of the Dodecanese Islands and, in fact, would eventually wrest control of Los and Leros islands. Probably because they expected greater support than they got from their allies, the British decided to hold Leros. The 1st and 14th fighter groups were assigned to provide air support. The British naval units would use the name "Nostril"; the 14th Fighter Group, in particular, would garner special honors for the protection of the Royal Navy ships.

The 1st and 14th took off on October 4 for their destination in the Eastern Mediterranean known as Gambut. The 1st Fighter Group landed in good order, but the 14th had its own special bedlam as many of the P-38s were forced to land in pitch darkness. Luckily, the 14th was also brought down in good order except for four P-38s that landed on the hard desert near the airfield after being distracted by the lights of an isolated house. In the next days, the two P-38 groups would cover the fleet and carry out fighter-sweep missions.

It was during the patrol of October 9 that the commander of the 37th Fighter Squadron, Maj. William Leverette, brought a singular distinction to the 14th Fighter Group. Leverette was leading a flight of eight P-38s over the British ships when a formation of about twenty-five Ju 87s covered by twin-engine Ju 88s appeared to menace the fleet. Leaving three aircraft as top cover, Leverette led four other P-38s to attack the German formation. The German dive-bombers were completely disorganized by the fury of the attack and Leverette claimed six of them within a few minutes. Harry T. Hanna, who had never had a confirmed

Portrait of Bill Leverette as an aviation cadet (graduated March 23, 1940).   USAF

Leverette and Robert Margison, about the time of the Oct. 9, 1943, interception.   Ethell

victory before, claimed another five for instant acedom. 14th Fighter Group records also credit Lt. Homer Sprinkle with three Stukas and one each for Wayne Blue and Robert Margison.

When the tallies were finally made, Leverette was given credit for yet another German dive-bomber for a total of seven aircraft downed in a single flight. German records document only eight Stukas lost in the area during the time that this combat took place. Whether their claims were duplicated or evidence of a disastrous mission for the Stukas was simply lost during the war, Leverette and his pilots flew an outstanding escort and thoroughly disrupted a potentially crushing bombing attack.

The 14th Fighter Group commander recommended Leverette for the Medal of Honor in light of the fact that he had pressed the attack to the point of ramming one of the Stukas. Leverette finally received the next best award, the Distinguished Service Cross. It seems that the brass in the Mediterranean were extremely conservative with decorations, considering what airmen in other theaters did to rightfully win theirs. Nevertheless, Leverette's seven victories in a single mission is a record for the air war against the Germans.

By the end of October all P-38 units were transferred to the newly formed Fifteenth Air Force. Lightnings had taken the brunt of the action in North Africa and in consequence had suffered the greatest casualties and earned the most victories. Thirty-seven Americans had become aces in P-38s compared to twelve in Spitfires and ten in P-40s. "Dixie" Sloan's record of twelve victories remained the standard for the Twelfth Air Force. Flying against some of the best veterans of the Luftwaffe and Regia Aeronautica and often badly outnumbered, these pioneer P-38 aces set a standard to follow.

Harry T. Hanna receives the DFC for downing five Ju-87s and damaging a sixth. Note Hanna's non-standard uniform items.   USAF

Oct. 17, 1943, on Olbia Field, Decimomannu. The three 14th F.G. squadron commanders: Leverette of the 37th, McKenzie of the 49th and Richardson of the 48th.

Chapter 9
Mediterranean War
Fifteenth Air Force

*E*SCORT WAS THE PRIMARY FUNCTION of P-38 units in the strategic Fifteenth Air Force. On one early mission flown on December 6, 1943, four German interceptors fell to Lightnings of the 82nd Fighter Group while the P-38s protected the B-24s over Athens. One P-38 was lost but Leslie Andersen claimed two of the Bf 109s to start his scoring. Four days later another nine fighters fell to the 82nd on an escort to Sofia, Bulgaria, and Andersen got his third victory. The 82nd was shocked, however, on Christmas day when six P-38s were lost over the Udine area in exchange for only one Bf 109.

Some veterans of the northwest European theater had derisively suggested that the German opposition on the Mediterranean front was inferior because about sixty percent of the entire Luftwaffe, including the crack fighter units, was deployed in the north. Col. Obie Taylor has suggested that, to the contrary, when weather prevented operations to the north, Fifteenth Air Force efforts faced the combined opposition of all Luftwaffe units—good, bad, or indifferent—that were stationed in the west.

December proved that Luftwaffe opposition in the Mediterranean could be brutal, wherever it came from, and also that the P-38 escort was equal to the task. The 14th Fighter Group saw a good deal of escort duty during the month and made some impressive scores. Since the 14th was to be moved to a Foggia base by the middle of December many targets were approachable over the entire range of southern Europe.

On the first day of December, Lt. Warren Jones of the 49th Squadron began his scoring by claiming a Bf 109 over Turin, Italy, during an escort of B-17s. Bill Leverette bridged the gap between the twelfth and fifteenth air forces by claiming his eighth victory when he caught a Bf 109 on a mission to Athens on December 14. Lt. Wilkins added a Messerschmitt to the pair of Ju 52s he claimed earlier when he caught the German fighter over Padua on December 16.

Evidence of the P-38 escort effectiveness became clear during December. During the first three weeks of December fewer than twenty heavy bombers and fewer than twenty-five P-38s were lost during twelve missions. In the same period the Lightning escort accounted for at least thirty-four enemy interceptors. The presence of the Lightning on

Leverette by his P-38H "Stingeree" after application of victory marks. (Stingeree is a southeastern U.S. variation of stingray.)   Bill Leverette

escort, even in limited numbers, made the Fifteenth Air Force bombing program completely supportable.

A climax of sorts came for the 14th Fighter Group on December 20, when the group escorted B-17s to Athens once again. Lt. Jack Lenox, Jr. was a neophyte combat pilot at the time and describes the action as he remembers it:

> . . . we spotted ME 109s attacking the last element of a B-17 group. We were at 28,000 and the ME 109s at about 22,000. The squadron leader gave the order to attack. I and Bob Seidman, the element leader, followed him in his dive to attack the enemy aircraft. During my dive I made a turn to the left to line up with one of the attacking ME 109s, losing sight of my leader. I observed black smoke trailing from the ME 109 I was firing at, but was unable to observe more as I continued my dive to outrun an ME 109 firing at me. Passing through about 15,000 feet, I was able to pull out of my dive and blacked out in the dive recovery. The next thing I knew, I was at 20,000 feet, alone, and trying to

Leverette displaying damaged propeller blade.

Leverette painting another swastika on his P-38 after downing a Messerschmitt 110 during a mission to Athens on Dec. 14, 1943.

find someone to attach myself to. Seeing another P-38 in the same predicament, I joined formation with the P-38 as his wing man and discovered it was the group commander.

When we returned home, Col. Taylor commented on how we had become involved in a fight, and although he was all over the sky, I had followed him and ended up in place on his wing. Of course I had no idea he was in the other P-38; all I was looking for was a wing to nest on.

During the battle, Col. Taylor jumped an Me 109, which became his first aerial victory. Taylor then had a difficult time pulling out of a screaming dive when his P-38 built up too much speed in the bounce. It's easy to see why Taylor might have been surprised to find Lenox still on his wing after the melee.

The top scorer of the day was Lt. Robert Seidman. Wanting to convey a message to his Nazi-oriented opponents, Seidman had painted a large Star of David on the nose of his P-38. Flashing through the German formation, he furiously attacked and sent crashing to earth three Bf 109s. Jack Lenox recalled that the comment Seidman made when he landed was something like, "I bet the huns would be real mad if they knew a little Hebrew boy had shot down three of their pilots today."

The secret of Seidman's success, according to some of those who flew with him, was his aggressive and determined nature. That nature may have been the cause of his downfall on a May 14, 1944, strafing mission over Villaorba airfield. After a punishing firing pass over the field, Seidman climbed suddenly to avoid high-tension wires, was caught in the flak pattern and went to his death when his P-38 was shot down.

Anzio was invaded on January 22, 1944, and consumed much of the Fifteenth Air Force's energy in the first months of the year. P-38s were heavily engaged and Don Kienholz, who had received the fright over the Salerno beaches the preceding autumn, scored his fifth victory over Anzio on January 24. His last claim fell on January 30.

Aces of the 14th Group were also active over Anzio. Bob Seidman destroyed another Messerschmitt for his fourth victory on January 27 and Max Wright of the 48th Squadron scored his first victory on January 30.

April saw the beginning of the escort operations under the 306th Fighter Wing with Fifteenth Air Force's full complement of seven fighter groups. The 14th Fighter Group earned its Distinguished Unit Citation on April 2 when it escorted the bombers back-from a strike on Steyr. The bombers had already been hammered by enemy fighters before the 14th arrived. When the P-38s finally did show up they found about seventy German and Italian interceptors making attacks.

Savage dogfights ensued with P-38s diving in and out of the battle on the tails of single and twin-engine fighters. The 1st and 82nd Fighter Groups had protected the B-17s and

Taylor and his crew in mid-1944.   Taylor

Taylor being readied for mission.   Taylor

B-24s on the approach and had claimed twelve interceptors between them for no losses. But the 14th had lost no P-38s and downed at least eighteen Axis aircraft before it was forced to break for home with a low fuel supply. John McGuyrt added a Bf 110 and an Italian RE2001 for part of the 48th Squadron's score that day, making his total, so far, four aerial victories.

May was another good month for the aces of the 14th Fighter Group. Lt. Warren Jones added a Bf 109 to his score on the 10th and claimed his fifth victory on the 25th. All five victories were Bf 109s.

Jack Lenox began his scoring on a mission over Ferrara, Italy, on May 23 when he claimed a Bf 109. The next day he nearly cashed in early on a mission to Hungary when a Bf 109 caught him from behind and shot his left engine out. Lenox had already shot down one Me 210 and was chasing another German when he was caught.

Lenox put his big fighter into some desperate maneuvers and fought to control it while he lost his pursuer in a dive. His canopy was shattered and, after he brought his Lightning out of its dive, for a brief moment he thought he was badly wounded. He gave himself a shot from the hypodermic in his emergency kit, but, shortly thereafter, he realized that what he believed was a paralyzed arm was simply his jacket caught on a throttle lock. Lenox made the rest of the flight home glad that his injuries were not serious but disgusted that he had given himself the injection unnecessarily.

Obie Taylor also claimed the last of his victories in May when he destroyed an Fw190 during a May 27 mission to Nimes-Serragia. During the next few weeks Taylor encountered another sort of enemy that was more effective than his Axis foes. In the summer of 1944 he was stricken with polio and was eventually relieved of his command to become medically retired. From the earliest days when the 14th Fighter Group almost dissolved into disgrace until the long trek up the Italian peninsula, Taylor had maintained an interest in the group and, as commander, had instilled a fighting spirit in the unit that led to a fine combat record. Col. Daniel Campbell took over in July.

The 82nd Fighter Group got a surprise visitor on May 27 when Louis Curdes returned as if from the dead. Curdes was officially listed as missing in action and was presumed dead. Some of the old hands in the group were pleasantly stunned and insisted on hearing what happened.

It seems that after he waited by the remains of his P-38 for some time the Italian Army came by to take him prisoner. Curdes quickly thought better of it and tried to escape only to be recaptured and thrown into prison. Seven months later he was ready to try again. Italy had surrendered after the Salerno landings and it was possible to reach friendly forces. This time Curdes remained free and found his way to the Allied lines. He was eventually sent home but went into combat again with the 3rd Air Com-

Thomas W. Smith of the 37th Fighter Squadron claimed a 109 the hard way when his P-38 rammed the German aircraft on Jan. 16, 1944, and Smith guided the wrecked Lightning home for a crashlanding.   IWM

Lt. Goldstein's P-38, name was repeated in German on starboard. 4 Air and 4 Ground victories. Goldstein-Graham

Herbert Hatch after his return from the Ploesti mission. The other pilots of the 71st Squadron may have been victims of Romanian fighters on that mission.   USAF

mando Group in the Pacific.

A special mission was carried out by the 82nd Fighter Group on June 10. With the 1st Fighter Group acting as top cover, the 82nd was scheduled to attack the formidable Ploesti oil refineries in Romania. The sprawling target proved as deadly as it had been on previous heavy bombing missions. This time it claimed twenty-three P-38s from the two groups.

Most of the Lightnings lost by the 82nd were downed by groundfire or collisions within the murky smoke clouds of burning refineries. German interceptors also claimed some of the P-38s by daring to enter the fiery maelstrom and challenge the raiders. Seven Germans fell to the guns of the 82nd including a persistent Bf 110, which Lt. Col. Ben Mason had to shoot down in self-defense. Other aircraft and rail targets were claimed on the ground by the group.

The 1st Fighter Group was having its own time of it against enemy fighters that were trying to get through to the bomb-carrying 82nd Fighter Group. A group of Romanian IAR 80 fighters managed to jump what must have been a formation of the 1st Fighter Group's 71st Squadron. Fourteen of the Lightnings were shot down when the enemy fighters caught them almost completely by surprise. The only 71st pilot to return home that night was Lt. Herbert

Hatch, who was given credit for five Fw190s during the engagement. In retrospect, it must have been the Romanian fighters that Hatch faced since the IAR 80 and the Fw190 are similar in appearance from the front.

Oddly enough, Hatch claimed his victories when a moment of hesitation caused him to turn in the opposite

Jack Lenox demonstrating his last victories before his P-38 "Snookie II."

Lenox via Ethell

direction from the rest of the 71st Squadron. While the other Lightnings turned away from the enemy, Hatch turned directly into them and simply shot down about five of the fighters before they could do the same to him. When Hatch landed at his base he wrote a letter home, not an exuberant letter about his phenomenal victory, but about his anxiety at the fate of his friends whom he hoped had landed safely, somewhere.

For all its cost to the attackers, the mission of June 10, 1944, was not really successful. Although a great deal of incidental damage was done, the refineries would be eliminated as a target only through several more weeks of heavy bombing. What the mission probably did accomplish was to draw to the oil complex more German air defense material, material that was in short supply elsewhere. In any event, the 82nd Fighter Group received its third DUC for the mission.

Four days after the Ploesti mission of June 10, the 49th Fighter Squadron of the 14th Fighter Group ran into a whirlwind of a dogfight. The bombers had already left the target at Petfurdo, Hungary, and the P-38s of the 49th were the only American aircraft in the area. As the Lightnings circled the area, some late-scrambling Messerschmitt 109s arrived on the scene and the general melee began. Jack Lenox turned his P-38 into the diving German fighters and shot down one Me 109 with a head-on burst.

Somehow, the American squadron became involved in a Lufberry circle with one P-38 following another. Lenox, having seen a P-38 under attack by two Germans, decided to break the maneuver and eased his fighter out of the circle to send one Me 109 down trailing heavy black smoke. Another Messerschmitt appeared in front of his P-38 and Lenox simply touched the trigger lightly to send the German down in flames for his third victory of the day and fifth total confirmed.

Lt. Louis Benne also claimed two of the Messerschmitts and achieved ace status. Unfortunately, Benne became a victory himself when another 109 shot out both his engines just seconds after Benne's last victory. Benne parachuted into captivity and had the rare privilege of meeting his victor when the enemy pilot visited the hospital where Benne's wounds were being treated. Four other P-38s were lost in the same battle.

The highest scoring P-38 ace of the Fifteenth Air Force began his string on July 8 when he caught an Me 109 over Austria. Capt. Michael Brezas was assigned to the 48th Squadron, 14th Fighter Group in May 1944; by the end of August he would have the remarkable tally of twelve German aircraft. Brezas was described as an enthusiastic and completely fearless airman who wanted to become a lawyer after the war. Unfortunately, he survived the war only to be killed in an F-86 accident in Korea.

The 82nd Fighter Group had a period of outstanding service in July. On July 5, the group set a Fifteenth Air Force record when it claimed its 500th air victory. Two days later on a fighter sweep over Vienna, 82nd pilots found a formation of sixteen German twin-engine fighters and downed all of them. Five other enemy planes were caught and downed on the same mission.

By August 15, 1944, Tom Maloney of the 1st had six air victories. His last two victories that day came during a wild dogfight:

... I led a dive-bombing mission of 12 planes, 4 each from the 27th, 71st and 94th squadrons just prior to H-Hour and I'm not sure, but I think we were the only allied aircraft to encounter enemy opposition that day. We were attacked by 8 Me-109s from above just as we were preparing to dive-bomb a railroad bridge some 50 miles NW of the beachhead. We had to jettison our bombs and turn our attention to the 109s and I saw Lt. Cecil Quesseth ... get the other 109 destroyed in a very beautiful shot and,

Maloney's crew chief by "Maloney's Pony" P-38L-1 s/n 44-34---, Sq #22, after Maloney was shot down. Photo dated September 1944.   Maloney

Charles Adams by his P-38 after the July 8, 1944, mission, during which he claimed 3 ME 410s.

via Steve Blake

at the same time, save Major Moorhead, an ace from the South Pacific who had joined our group . . .

I shot down one 109 on the original pass they made on us from above . . . I got the leader of their flight from headon . . . I continued the break around and down through a 450 [degree] turn, closing on the 2nd plane in their formation as the others seemed to go in several directions with some of our boys following. As I closed to firing position, I had just pressed the trigger, his canopy flew off and he bailed out at about 3000' . . . I saw a 109 in a shallow dive for the ground (rough terrain) with a P-38 about 500 yards behind and closing. This was Major Moorhead. Almost immediately, I saw a 109 from a slightly steeper angle falling in behind the P-38 and closing much faster. I called the break but Major Moorhead had started shooting from a distance and didn't break. Quesseth came from I don't know where and made the 4th plane in the string. I continued to call for the break by 71st Squadron (I didn't know who the pilot was but I could identify the squadron

by color). Maj. Moorhead at this point realized he was being shot at as he started a loop off the deck (I couldn't believe it). The 109 shot at him all the way up and just as the 109 reached 145 [degrees] of the loop, Quesseth overtook him and on an excellent tough deflection shot, blew up the 109. All this time, I was doing my best to get close enough to help. This all took place in about 1/10th the time it took you to read this.

Four days later, Tom Maloney took off on his last mission; he would not return until he had written a page in the history of personal courage and devotion to duty. Maloney had already flown a patrol mission to Toulon on the morning of August 19 and was scheduled to fly a dive-bombing sortie to Avignon in the afternoon. The 94th Squadron leader threw caution to the wind as a long, unprotected train was sighted just northwest of Marseilles. The P-38 squadron made a great circle over the target and each fighter made

pass after pass on the train. Maloney seemed to strike something explosive on every pass and once he even saw rolling stock blasted as high as his own aircraft. Returning from the strike, Maloney noticed an oil leak in first one engine and then the other. Maloney was inevitably forced to ditch his fighter into the Mediterranean and began a long and painful adventure.

Frustration began right away for the disconsolate pilot sitting in his rubber life raft and bobbing on the unusually rough surface of the Mediterranean. Although six planes from his squadron circled above and Maloney was sure that

the word was out to pick him up, nobody appeared until dusk. After the guarding P-38s had to leave him alone in the water, rescue ships finally arrived. They managed to pass within a few hundred feet of the frantically waving pilot and miss him completely. When the ships departed, Maloney noticed he was drifting toward shore and decided to make for the beach.

Maloney was not certain what he would find on shore. The invasion of southern France had begun only days before and the position of Allied lines was unclear. However, he had not gone more than fifty feet up the beach when

14th Fighter Group over Weiheim Marshalling yards on April 19, 1945. Top 14th F.G. locomotive aces were Lt. Cols. Charles D. Chitty and Hugh A. Griffith with over thirty engines each. During February and March 1945, 14th Fighter Group destroyed 290 locomotives.   USAF

he heard a noise that sounded like a rifle being cocked. Maloney froze and, in a fraction of a second, realized in horror what that sound was. A moment later, the land mine exploded with a roar, hurling Maloney into the gray sand.

Tom Maloney is one of the more fortunate survivors and evaders of World War II. He described the next ten days:

There are few if any participants in World War II who were luckier than I am to be alive. By all odds, there was no reason for me to survive. Both my legs were compound fractured, both feet were shattered, my left knee had several large pieces of metal in the middle of the joint. I had gaping holes on both upper and lower legs in addition to the breaks. A piece of metal cut through my right bicep numbing my arm. My face was torn by schrapnel and was powder-burned. My pants were torn off 6" below the waist . . . When I landed on my side from the blast, my left shoe was still on and I remember suffering an unbearable hot-foot. I tried to remove the shoe but a piece of jagged metal had impaled the foot in the shoe . . . My escape kit was still attached to my belt and I hastily undid it and used the pitifully small amount of sulfa ointment on some of my wounds and then passed out.

Second day: I awoke the next morning and, of course, was all alone. I tried to get a drink from the canteen in my escape kit but it was empty. I would alternately pass out and wake up.

Third day: It became apparent to me I was going to die of thirst if not from my wounds and I started moving toward a two or three foot rise with a row of bushes on top. It was about fifty feet away and I would pick up one leg, set it down, then the other, being careful not to hit another mine or trip wire. Since I still was only conscious for short periods of time, it took me several periods of consciousness to move the fifty feet . . . On the other side of the rise was a six inch deep pool of trapped water which was so very welcome . . . I spent that nite and the next day by the edge of that pool and, as before, was unconscious most of the time.

Fifth day: I tried to raise my head as far as possible and see if there was anything around me that I might try to reach for help. To the East of me I could see the top of a tall wooden observation tower . . . I thought surely it would be manned and by this time, I would have welcomed a German . . . By the end of the fifth day, I hadn't made much progress and simply slept where I was.

Sixth day: I continued to move myself toward the tower and got to within 100 yards by nightfall on the sixth day. There was a swamp between me and the tower and by now I could see there was a log cabin which appeared to be a hunting cabin at the base of the tower and both were obviously abandoned.

Seventh day: I entered the swamp which turned out to be about 2 to 4 feet deep variable and I was able to move quite well in this because my legs were aided by the buoyancy . . . I pulled myself to the cabin cautiously as there were signs in German, "Achtung! Minen," and I knew what that meant.

During the next two days, Maloney labored to build a raft from material that he found at the cabin but again he met with frustration as the swamp led only to blind alleys. Returning to the cabin, he was finally rescued by friendly Frenchmen, who attempted to bind Maloney's wounds. A Canadian soldier who happened to be in the area finally brought help from American units nearby and Maloney's ordeal was ended. Members of his group who visited Maloney in the hospital were amazed that someone in his condition could have survived at all, let alone traverse the obstacles he faced in those swamps of southern France. Tom Maloney's experience must stand as a classic in stamina and personal determination.

The months that followed saw an ebb in activity for the Mediterranean P-38s. During September, no enemy aircraft were even spotted by the Lightning units. The 82nd Fighter Group, which had held the high-scoring honors for all Fifteenth Air Force Fighter units with over 550 confirmed victories, gave way to the 31st Fighter Group on March 31, 1945, when that unit claimed nearly thirty enemy planes to reach the 560 mark. Affection for the P-38 had not waned with the bomber crews, however, as might be evinced by this bit of doggerel composed by an anonymous radioman on a Fifteenth Air Force B-17:

Oh, Hedy Lamarr is a beautiful gal
and Madeleine Carroll is too,
But you'll find if you query, a different theory
amongst any bomber crew
For the loveliest thing of which one could sing
(this side of the pearly gates)
Is no blonde or brunette of the Hollywood set—
But an escort of P-38s.

Yes, in the days that have passed, when the tables were
   massed
with glasses of scotch and champagne,
It's quite true that the sight was a thing to delight
Us, intent upon feeling no pain.
But no longer the same, nowadays, in this game
When we head north from Messina Straits
Take the sparkling wine—every time just make mine
an escort of P-38s.

Byron, Shelley and Keats ran a dozen dead heats
Describing the view from the hills,
of the valleys in May when the winds gently sway
In the air it's a different story;
We sweat out our track through the fighter and flak
We're willing to split up the glory
Well, they wouldn't reject us, so Heaven protect us
and, until all this shooting abates,
Give us courage to fight 'em—one other small item—
An escort of P-38s.

Chapter Ten
The Top Aces

THERE WERE FIVE P-38 PILOTS WHO scored at least twenty air-to-air victories. They all served with the Fifth Air Force, and, of course, scored all their victories against Japanese aircraft. In Europe, only three P-38 pilots claimed more than ten German and Italian aircraft. Michael Brezas had a spectacular scoring bout as may be witnessed from the selected tallies included in the appendix. "Dixie" Sloan registered steadily against the Luftwaffe and Regia Aeronautica during the spring and summer of 1943 and William Leverette has already been discussed concerning his remarkable victory.

This chapter will deal primarily with those pilots who managed to down about twenty enemy aircraft. It should be kept in mind that the victory lists following discussion of each pilot were gleaned largely from each pilot's combat report and might therefore be subject to revision. Less than certain information is duly qualified.

Richard Ira Bong

Dick Bong was perhaps the epitome of the American idea of what a hero should be. Usually happy and in high spirits, the ebullient Bong was brimming with enthusiasm and optimism. Until the time of his death in the unfortunate P-80 accident, he remained unaffected by his reputation or the heady realization that he was the top American fighter ace of the war. Bong was always given to simple pleasures and modest tastes in the tradition of the rural American Midwest.

If he did have a passion it was the P-38 fighter that he flew. At the time that he broke Rickenbacker's record he maintained that he was a "one airplane man, and that airplane was the P-38." By April of 1945 he had flown a number of types including the A-20, B-25, P-40, P-47, P-51, P-61, P-63 and, of all things, the OA-10 Catalina. Of course, the only airplane he had ever flown on combat operations was the P-38 but he still preferred it because of its twin-engine safety and reliable performance, its sparkling climb, firepower and range.

The controversy in the southwest Pacific over the rel-

ative merits of the P-38 and the P-47 came to a head during a legendary mock combat between Bong and Col. Neel Kearby. Kearby was just as keen on the P-47 as Bong was about the P-38. Around August 1, 1943, the two pilots were reputed to have settled the matter in the skies over Port Moresby in a friendly competition with hundreds of witnesses on the ground. The general concensus seems to be that the contest was very close but testimony from some of the pilots of Bong's old 9th Fighter Squadron seems to give him the winning edge.

Bong was born in Poplar, Wisconsin, on September 24, 1920. He was a student at Superior State College when he became an aviation cadet on May 29, 1941. Graduating with class 42-A on January 9, 1942, he was an instructor at Luke Field before being assigned to the Fourth Air Force at

Maj. Richard I. Bong in his dress tans.

Dick Bong during his training days in the air over the Grand Canyon in an AT-6.

Bong at far left with classmates, (class 42 A), by PT-17.

Hamilton Field under General Kenney. Bong became well acquainted with Kenney under less than happy circumstances when he was hauled into the general's office for violations of strict air regulations. Bong was a free spirit in the air, following in the best tradition of unruly Army Air cadets. Kenney read the riot act to Bong but somehow sensed the emerging potential in the young fighter pilot and made sure that he was included in the first group of P-38 people sent out to the Pacific. Bong was in New Guinea by November and in action within a month.

One of the most successful missions that Bong flew came on July 26, 1943, when he claimed two Tonys and two Oscars. Dick was famous for his terse combat reports and this might serve as an example:

> I was leader of blue flight when we were scrambled to Salamaua dropping area at 1230/K. We went up there and made a circle over Lae and came down to Salamaua and then went down the Markham Valley. There were about 20 fighters, 10 inline engine fighters and 10 Zeros. I dropped my tanks and shot at an inline job and missed. I dove out and shot at a Zero head-on and he burst into

flames. I shot at an inline job 45 degrees from behind and above and knocked peices [sic] off his fuselage. I shot at another inline job and he burst into flames. I shot at another Zero head-on and knocked pieces out of his canopy and engine cowling or engine. Shot at one more inline job and missed. I left the area at 1410/K and returned to the base and landed.

Some veterans have suggested that their probable victories were more certain than the confirmed. To some extent the same may be said of Bong's victories. Whenever he saw a Japanese aircraft going down after he attacked and no witnesses or gun camera film were available the claim would be a simple probable. Nobody ever tried to question or prove a probable. When a pilot said he probably shot a Japanese plane down it was accepted with no question.

On the other hand, if the attack was witnessed, every effort would be made to gather evidence and prove that the enemy aircraft could not possibly survive. One example of Bong's probables came on September 6, 1943, when he claimed two Betty bombers on a patrol over Morobe. Bong was in a formation of fifteen 9th Squadron P-38s about 16,000 feet high at 1:45 p.m. when he called out the thirty Bettys and Zeros:

> I made a quarter tail attack on one Betty and got in a long burst. This bomber immediately started smoking badly and dropped out of formation, losing altitude rapidly. I made a pass from the stern of another Betty, and observed hits along the fuselage and both wings. This bomber started smoking heavily and dropped out of formation, losing altitude rapidly. Lieutenant PRICE saw both of these bombers at 4,000 feet, smoking badly and still going down. The combat took place at 14,000 feet.

These victories were never confirmed for Bong although Theron Price, who flew Bong's wing that day, verified that both aircraft fell smoking into the clouds at 4,000 feet. Other of Bong's victories that were confirmed

Gun camera still attributed to Dick Bong sometime in 1943.   USAF

-100-

Dick Bong with Generals Whitehead (left) and Wurtsmith. AFM

Bong gives his bride, Marge, a ride in the P-38.

Bong and USAAF officers by P-38 used for publicity purposes in the U.S.

Bong in the cockpit of s/n 42-104380, marked with twenty-seven victories.

did not have quite so much evidence in support. There is no doubt that Bong downed at least forty Japanese aircraft but his official list is arbitrary at best and is an approximate guide to his successes. The same is true for most official victory lists.

General Kenney had reported that the first time Bong ever became aware that he was engaged in a grisly business was on an afternoon in late December 1944 when the pilot of a doomed Zero over an American base jumped to escape the flames and landed in a gory mass practically at the feet of Kenney and Bong who were watching the air battle between P-38s and Japanese. Bong became ill at the sight and Kenney was certain that the incident had a profound effect on Bong's mental attitude for he morosely refused the controls of any airplane during the next few days.

One fact that should be made clear is that the only

source for this incident was General Kenney. Dick never indicated to his family in his letters or his speech that he had been affected thusly by such an unpleasant occurrence. However, if General Kenney was right in his assessment, the tragic manner of the ace's own death takes on ironic character.

It was on a bright day—in fact the day of the atomic bombing of Hiroshima, August 6, 1945—that residents of a southern California neighborhood heard the anguished rush of a P-80 jet fighter in distress at low altitude. There was no doubt that the airplane was doomed to crash and one of the people who observed the falling jet saw the pilot vault out of the cockpit with his arms raised high above his head. The pilot disappeared behind some of the buildings and the people on the ground were horrified to realize that his parachute had not opened. The aircraft had fortunately crashed and burst into flame on open ground, causing little damage. It was only after the fire was extinguished and the wreckage collected that the identity of the pilot began to be made known. Maj. Richard Ira Bong, the victor of a hundred desperate air battles, was tragically and, in view of General Kenney's assessment, ironically killed in that aircraft accident.

Besides winning the Medal of Honor, Bong was awarded the DSC, twice the Silver Star, seven DFCs and fifteen Air Medals. Even a cursory glance at his victory list suggests that he was brave and aggressive enough to have thoroughly earned each decoration.

Maj. Thomas Buchanan McGuire by "Pudgy (V)" in December 1944.   Glen Cooper

Richard Ira Bong Victory List

No.	Date	Place	Aircraft Downed
1, 2	27 Dec 42	Dobodura	1 Zero, 1 Val
3, 4	7 Jan 43	Huon Gulf	2 Oscars
5	8 Jan 43	Lae Harbor	1 Oscar
6	3 Mar 43	Huon Gulf	1 Oscar
7, 8	11 Mar 43	Bismarck Sea	2 Zeros
9	29 Mar 43	Bismarck Sea	1 Dinah
10	14 Apr 43	Milne Bay	1 Betty
11	12 Jun 43	Bona Bona	1 Oscar
12-15	26 Jul 43	NW of Lae	2 Tonys, 2 Oscars
16	28 Jul 43	Rein Bay	1 Oscar
17	2 Oct 43	Gasmata	1 Dinah
18, 19	29 Oct 43	Rabaul	2 Zeros
20, 21	5 Nov 43	Rabaul	2 Zeros
22	15 Feb 44	Cape Hoskins	1 Tony
23, 24	3 Mar 44	Tadji	2 Sallys
25	3 Apr 44	Hollandia	1 Oscar
26-28	12 Apr 44	Hollandia	3 Oscars
29, 30	10 Oct 44	Balikpapan	1 Nick, 1 Oscar
31	27 Oct 44	Tacloban	1 Oscar
32, 33	28 Oct 44	Masbate	2 Oscars
34	10 Nov 44	Ormoc Bay	1 Oscar
35, 36	11 Nov 44	Ormoc Bay	2 Zeros
37, 38	7 Dec 44	Ormoc Bay	1 Tojo, 1 Sally
39	15 Dec 44	Penubulon	1 Oscar
40	17 Dec 44	Mindoro	1 Oscar

Thomas Buchanan McGuire

Born in Ridgewood, New Jersey, in 1920, McGuire went down to Georgia Tech in 1937 to major in mechanical engineering. His interest in aviation started in 1940 when he learned to fly Piper Cubs at Candler Field, Florida. He enlisted in the Army on July 12, 1941, as an aviation cadet and completed his primary pilot training at Corsicana, Texas, in September. He then went to Randolph for basic pilot training and then to Kelly Field, where he completed advanced training in February, 1942.

Dennis Glen Cooper made McGuire take off his disreputable service hat. Mac must have felt naked.   Glen Cooper

McGuire was not happy with his assignment at Key Field, Mississippi, flying P-35s with the 50th Pursuit Group. He asked for overseas duty and eventually wound up with the 54th Fighter Group in Alaska. Little happened in the way of excitement until he was ordered to fly to Anchorage and was lost in a blizzard. His entire flight of five P-39s landed in a patch of tundra and the pilots walked out of the area with the help of supplies dropped by air.

Then came the historic introduction of Tom McGuire and the P-38. He had his first check-out flight on February 16, 1943, but the result was not auspicious. The P-38 canopy collapsed during takeoff and knocked Mac senseless. By March 7, however, McGuire and the P-38 were acquainted well enough to begin their famed partnership.

On March 14, 1943, McGuire left the United States and was assigned first to the 9th Fighter Squadron and then, on July 20, to the 431st Fighter Squadron.

The fact that McGuire scored only single victories on occasion was largely due to the lack of targets or some prior commitment to bomber escort duties. An example of the latter case is evident in McGuire's report for the mission of May 19, 1944:

We took off from Hollandia drome at 1120/K, rendez-vousing with the bombers off the west of Japan Island. I was leading Red flight of Hades and we arrived over the target at 1335/K. Flak was of heavy calibre, heavy intensity and accurate, bursting between 14,000 and 18,000 feet. At 1340/K we made contact with the enemy consisting of a flight of one Tojo and three probable Oscars just west of Manokwari. We dropped tanks and started for them. The Nips were diving from above and to the left and ahead of our formation. We slipped in behind them. Picking out the element leader I opened fire with a short burst and followed him until he stalled out going straight up and rolling slightly. I then fired another short burst hitting him in the cockpit. There was a flash of flame and then the Tojo started down and almost immediately exploded. The pilot was blown clear and parachuted down. I then started down after the others; there were approximately eight E/A in all. When the bombers called that there were some E/A near, we returned to them and covered them back to Tydeman Reefs, where we left the bombers and returned home, landing at 1600/K. The Japs flew standard U.S. formation. Tojo had dark camouflage and the pilot seemed experienced.

It was perhaps McGuire's aggressive nature that caused him to be frustrated with Bong's easy natural ability as a fighter pilot. The two pilots reportedly never got along very well and McGuire was perhaps the only person able to ruffle Bong's calm exterior. McGuire's aggressiveness served well when he became commander of the 431st Fighter Squadron on May 2, 1944. The 475th thrived on strict squadron leaders and McGuire let none make the mistake that he was an exception. By the time of his death in combat, McGuire had tallied thirty-eight confirmed victories.

The manner of his death indicates that he was a fine fighter and leader.

Thomas Buchanan McGuire Victory List

No.	Date	Place	Aircraft Type
1-3.	18 Aug 43	Wewak	2 Zeros, 1 Tony
4, 5	21 Aug 43	Wewak	2 Zeros
6, 7	29 Aug 43	Wewak	1 Zero, 1 Tony
8, 9	28 Sep 43	Wewak	2 Zeros
10	15 Oct 43	Oro Bay	1 Val
11-13	17 Oct 43	Oro Bay	3 Zeros
14-16	26 Dec 43	Cape Gloucester	3 Vals
17	17 May 44	Biak	1 Oscar
18	19 May 44	Manokwari	1 Tojo
19, 20	16 Jun 44	Jefman	1 Oscar, 1 Sonia
21	27 Jul 44	Lolobata	1 Oscar
22-24	14 Oct 44	Balikpapan	1 Oscar, 1 Hamp, 1 Tojo
25	1 Nov 44	Leyte	1 Tojo
26	10 Nov 44	Ormoc Bay	1 Oscar
27, 28	12 Nov 44	Cebu	2 Jacks
29, 30	7 Dec 44	Ormoc Bay	1 Oscar, 1 Tojo
31	13 Dec 44	Negros	1 Jack
32-34	25 Dec 44	Clark Field (Mabalacat)	3 Zeros
35-38	26 Dec 44	Clark Field	4 Zeros

Charles Henry MacDonald

Born and raised in DuBois, Pennsylvania, Colonel MacDonald went to college at Louisiana State University from 1935 to 1938. He was interested in all the sciences and especially philosophy and got his Bachelor of Arts in 3½ years. He enlisted as a flying cadet at Randolph Field in 1938 and took his primary and basic flight training there. He went on to advanced training at Kelly Field where he trained in fighters. After finishing at Kelly in 1939 he was assigned to the 20th Pursuit Group at Barksdale Field in Louisiana.

MacDonald became a regular second lieutenant during his training when he easily passed the test for a commission in the Regular Army. By the time his new commission came through he moved to California in preparation for his group to be assigned to Hawaii. In February 1941, forty P-36s were loaded aboard the aircraft carrier *Enterprise* and MacDonald's group sailed to Hawaii. He subsequently had a unique experience for an Army pilot—flying off the deck of an aircraft carrier. Assigned to Hawaii for the next two years, he was witness to the Pearl Harbor attack.

McGuire on the wing of his P-38. Photo dated Jan. 5, 1945, just two days before Mac was killed.

National Archives

Early in 1943 he returned to the mainland and attended the Orlando Fighter Command School. During this time MacDonald was promoted to major. He also took command of the 340th Fighter Squadron at the New York Defense Wing and trained a new crew of Thunderbolt pilots. He went with the 340th and the rest of the 348th Fighter Group to Port Moresby, New Guinea, in June 1943. From the end of July through September he flew uneventful missions covering transports in the Marilinan area.

If the assignment to the 340th was discouraging to MacDonald, he got his chance in October when he was assigned to the 475th as an executive officer.

On October 15, 1943, during the big Japanese raid on Oro Bay, MacDonald sat up and realized that here was his opportunity to get his first shots at the Japanese. He took Captain Ivey with him as wingman and confiscated two P-38s from the 433rd Squadron. The two airplane thieves pointed their fighters in the direction of the enemy and found them around 8 a.m. at sea level in the Oro Bay area.

MacDonald managed to be ahead of everyone and attacked seven Vals by himself. One Val that he attacked from the rear hit the water and exploded. He started another Val smoking, which Captain Ivey then attacked and caused to crash. MacDonald then had his head of steam up and damaged another Val in a head-on pass. He shot at another dive-bomber from the rear and watched it explode just as he passed ahead of it.

During a subsequent attack on yet another Val, Mac-Donald was bounced by a Hamp, which fired some accurate bursts and put out the P-38's left engine, electrical system, hydraulics and holed the fuel tanks. MacDonald had to crash-land at Dobodura and the P-38 was written off

but he and Ivey laughed like madmen at the four definites and two probables they claimed between them.

MacDonald then quickly claimed an Oscar over Rabaul on October 23 and a Zero over the same area two days later. He became an ace on November 9 during the same mission to Alexishafen that claimed Danny Roberts. MacDonald filed his report with the 432nd Fighter Squadron:

Col. Charles H. MacDonald.

Maj. Charles H. MacDonald when he commanded the 340th F.S.
G.R. Roberts

MacDonald returned home in mid-1945 and remained in the Air Force until he retired in 1966 with the rank of colonel. For some time he remained a recluse, either cruising the ocean or living in Costa Rica. His old comrades in the 475th were delighted, however, when the shy commander relented and attended a recent group reunion.

One final note about Colonel MacDonald concerns some comments that he made to the author recently. I asked him about some statement that he made to the effect that if the Japanese had P-38s and the 475th had Zeros, tactics would have made the 475th winners anyway. He responded that he probably did make the comment but that the P-38 was his favorite fighter and far better than other types he had flown, including the P-47 with the 348th Fighter Group. He liked the visibility and climb most of all, but said that the armament and speed of the Lightning were also strong points.

With that sort of endorsement it is easy to see why the P-38 was dominant in the southwest Pacific. MacDonald proved his point at least twenty-seven times and remains the top-scoring P-38 pilot to survive the war.

Ten to fifteen enemy fighters were attacked after the last B-25 made his run. I made an identification pass on a Zeke, didn't fire, but told the rest of the flight to get him. Lt. Rundell did, and I saw the Zeke crash in flames. I got a slight deflection shot on another Zeke and fired a long burst. He fell out of control and crashed into the sea. I mixed it with three more Zekes and got two cannon holes in the tail, one in my boom, and some .50 cal. in the wing. I got on the tail of one Zeke who was diving for the strip at Alexishafen. I closed to minimum range and fired a long burst into him. He began coming apart, flaming, and crashed into the strip. About this time I saw a P-38 burning, the booms came apart, and he crashed on the shore.

Lt. Condon and I came down the Markham Valley alone after the above engagement, and noticing a dogfight over Nadzab, climbed up and attacked a group of three Oscars. I made a head-on pass at one who dove away, and a P-39 hit him with his cannon. The tail fell off and the Nip tumbled down. I then made another head-on pass at an Oscar, and fired a long burst into his engine and cockpit. We came so close that the shock of air threw my left wing up. When I looked back he was disappearing into low cumulus. He was falling out of control. He went straight down and was so low he should not have pulled out. It was impossible to see him crash because of the clouds. He may have crashed three or four miles NW. of Nadzab strip. Lt. Condon witnessed this action.

I also saw a parachute which looked as if it would land just south of Nadzab. We stayed in the area about ten minutes—no further sightings, so we returned to Dobodura.

I claim two (2) enemy Zeke type airplanes definitely destroyed and one enemy type Oscar airplane probably destroyed.

Charles Henry MacDonald Victory List

No.	Date	Place	Aircraft Type
1, 2	15 Oct 43	Oro Bay	2 Vals
3	23 Oct 43	SW Rabaul	1 Oscar
4	25 Oct 43	Vunakanau, Rabaul	1 Zero
5,6	9 Nov 43	Alexishafen	2 Zeros
7,8	21 Dec 43	N. of Arawe, New Britain	2 Vals
9	10 Jan 44	Boram	1 Tony
10	18 Jan 44	N. of Wewak	1 Hamp
11	18 Jun 44	60 miles NW of Manokwari	1 Zero
13	1 Aug 44	Koror Island	1 Rufe, 1 Val
14	10 Nov 44	Ormoc Bay	1 Oscar
15,16	11 Nov 44	S.E. Ormoc Bay	2 Jacks
17	28 Nov 44	Ormoc Bay	1 Zero
18-20	7 Dec 44	Ormoc Bay	2 Zeros, 1 Jack
21	13 Dec 44	W. Mindanao Sea	1 Sally
22-24	25 Dec 44	N. of Mabalacat Field	2 Jacks, 1 Zero
25, 26	1 Jan 45	Clark Field	1 Dinah, 1 Tojo
27	13 Feb 45	South China Sea	1 Topsy

General Wurtsmith and Colonel MacDonald sometime in mid-1944.   Gregg

McGuire, Lindbergh, Meryl Smith and MacDonald in the summer of 1944.   Dennis Glen Cooper

MacDonald and Lindbergh by "Putt-Putt Maru" sometime in mid-1944   Dennis Glen Cooper

Gerald Richard Johnson

Known as "Johnny Eager," Johnson was one of the most exuberant fighter pilots in the Army Air Forces. He took any mission for the chance of aerial combat and he was just as frisky in routine flight. One of his flying comrades claims to have seen Johnson loop a P-38 with both engines feathered. Other legendary stories claim that Johnson did the same thing with a B-25, another airplane that he favored.

In point of fact, Johnson and Bong were among the most enthusiastic champions of the P-38. While Bong liked the P-38 for things like its speed and ability to fly on a single engine, Johnson apparently went one better and turned off both engines. At one point in the New Guinea campaign Johnson and Neel Kearby of the P-47 equipped 348th Fighter Group debated so heatedly the merits of P-38 vs. P-47 that they decided to settle the matter with a mock combat over Port Moresby. As it turned out, Kearby finally had the mock battle with Dick Bong on August 1, 1943, and the results were generally regarded to be inconclusive.

Johnson's impulsiveness even extended to combat situations. Sometimes that impulsiveness displayed itself in acts of chivalry like the gesture he made during the August 2, 1943, engagement. A similar incident happened while Johnson and a Japanese pilot were tearing at each other in a head-on dogfight. Both men ran out of ammunition at the same time and were able to draw alongside each

Gerald Johnson as an aviation cadet.   USAF

other, virtually unable to do damage. Both pilots offered a salute to the other man before flying on in opposite directions.

Johnson continued on during the occupation of Japan and could be seen flying a P-38, P-51 or B-25 over the once-again peaceful skies of the home islands. It was another impetuous act that brought about his death on October 7, 1945. The weather was dangerous and threatening between Okinawa and Honshu but Johnson decided to try and beat the odds and piled three passengers aboard his B-25 to make it back to the Tokyo area. Winds reached typhoon proportions and the entire coast became socked in. Johnson gave the three parachutes aboard the aircraft to the passengers and they bailed out to safety. Johnson and his co-pilot were not so lucky. Their bodies washed up on a Japanese beach a few weeks later.

One of the battles that justified Johnson's nickname came during a fight on October 23, 1943, over Rabaul's Blanche Bay. He described the incident in his combat report:

> . . . We dropped our belly tanks and my flight dived ahead to the attack. I turned to the left, diving after a Zeke that had completed a pass near 10 B-24 s. I cut my throttles back and fired from dead astern. Two bright explosions occurred and his tail disintegrated. The pieces came back and put nicks in my wings and prop hubs. He rolled over and went straight in.
>
> . . . Captain Haney & Lts. Johnson, S.W., & Swift observed me making a pass at the first enemy airplane and saw it explode and large pieces fly off. They will confirm this claim.
>
> I claim one (1) Zeke definitely destroyed.

Gerald R. Johnson, probably about the time that he served in the Aleutians, autumn 1942-winter 1943.

Barbara Curtis

Gerald Richard Johnson Victory List

No.	Date	Place	Aircraft Type
1	25 Sep 42*	Kiska-Adak	1 Zero
2	1 Oct 42*	Kiska-Adak	1 Zero
3, 4	26 Jul 43	NW of Lae	1 Oscar, 1 Tony
5	2 Sep 43	NW of Cape Gloucester	1 Nick
6-8	15 Oct 43	NE of Oro Bay	2 Vals, 1 Oscar
9	23 Oct 43	Blanche Bay, Rabaul	1 Zero
10, 11	2 Nov 43	NE of Rabaul	2 Zeros
12	10 Dec 43	20 miles N of Gusap	1 Tony
13	18 Jan 44	Wewak	1 Zero
14, 15	14 Oct 44	Balikpapan, Borneo	1 Tojo, 1 Oscar
16, 17	27 Oct 44	Tacloban	1 Oscar, 1 Val
18, 19	11 Nov 44	Ormoc Bay	2 Zeros
20-23	7 Dec 44	S. of Ormoc Bay	3 Oscars, 1 Helen
24	2 Apr 45	N. of Hong Kong	1 Tojo

*Some lists omit the two claims that Johnson made while flying P-39s in the Aleutians. Headquarters, Fifth Air Force, granted the victories to Johnson. According to that command, Johnson scored two victories with the P-39, two with the P-47 and twenty with the P-38.

Jay Thorpe Robbins

One of the more thoroughly effective fighter pilots of World War II, Robbins had the distinction of claiming four victories in a single engagement on two separate occasions. During both occasions he closed with large numbers of Japanese fighters and cooly shot them down even though he was outnumbered. Over Rabaul, on October 24, 1943, he even faced a resolute pilot in a Zero or Hamp and shot him down despite what appeared to be an attempt by the enemy pilot to ram Robbins' P-38.

Robbins was born on September 16, 1919, in Coolidge, Texas, and graduated from Coolidge High School in 1936. He got his Bachelor of Science degree from Texas A&M University in 1940 and was granted a commission as second lieutenant through his ROTC participation. He began flight training at Corsicana, Texas, in mid-1941 and received his wings in July 1942.

Robbins was among the first generation of 80th Fighter Squadron aces, assigned to that squadron in September 1942. He became first squadron commander after the loss of Ed Cragg and later deputy group com-

Johnson in the cockpit of his P-38 in 1943.

Harry Brown

Jay. T. Robbins in formal portrait.   AFM

Jerry Johnson by "Duckbutt" Watkins' "Charlcie Jeanne."

mander during the initial days of the Philippines invasion in 1944. He first came to grips with the Japanese while the 80th was flying P-39 aircraft on January 17, 1943. He missed being credited an air victory by the toss of a coin when he and another pilot had to settle who would be granted credit for a bomber at which they both had shot.

He scored his first victories when he was escorting B-25s with the rest of the 80th Fighter Squadron over Bogadjim. He was just leaving the target when Robbins noticed enemy fighters closing from the rear. He had just enough time to turn his P-38 into the attack and shoot one of the Japanese down and then noticed another P-38 under attack. He shot the pursuer off his squadronmate's tail, but couldn't claim a definite kill because more Japanese dived to the attack. Robbins twisted his P-38 and turned to defend other Americans under attack, claiming two more Zeros (probably the Japanese fighters were actually Oscars, considering the area of combat). He left the combat only when his P-38 ran low on fuel.

This combat could have been Robbins' last; a routine physical discovered an irregularity in his heartbeat. He would normally have been disqualified from combat flying, but Robbins was not quite through yet and demanded a waiver. It could have been an added danger for him, but he continued flying combat and rolled up a distinguished record in the process. Nobody who could ever have done something about it learned about Robbins' physical disqualification.

As it was, his twentieth victory was scored within the next year. His combat report of the day relates some of the excitement of the situation:

Robbins in early shot with his new P-38.

"Cock" Robbins poses in his P-38.   AFM

Robbins planning mission with pilots of the 80th F.S.
(Note P-38 "W" in background.)

I was leading the 80th Fighter Squadron with 13 P-38s as top cover; we reached the rendezvous point at 1130 and continued to target. We reached the target area at 1255 and about this time saw several enemy fighters taking off from Jefman. After careful observation above we dropped tanks and made wide sweeping turns downward. A SONIA was my first target but I only damaged it. After two other deflection shots, I set fire to a ZEKE. He burst into flames on the right wing root and went in from about two-hundred feet just south of Samate. I called the squadron to join up and head for home but only one pilot could find me; we turned and headed for base at 6,000 ft. and I noticed Zeke heading for Jefman. I turned toward him and several other P-38s made passes as well. He headed toward the shore line doing slow rolls and steep turns at low altitude and finally went into a cloud. I followed him, almost colliding with a plane from the 432nd Squadron as I entered the cloud. I made a right turn and broke out of the cloud and saw the Zeke in front of me and heading away. I fired a long burst and he caught on fire in the left wing. He did a slow roll to the left and crashed into a mountain . . .

Jay Robbins retired from the Air Force as a Lieutenant General in the early 1970s.

Jay Thorpe Robbins Victory List

No.	Date	Place	Aircraft Type
1-3	21 Jul 43	Bogadjim, N.G.	3 Zeros
4-7	4 Sep 43	Huon Gulf, N.G.	4 Zeros
8-11	24 Oct 43	Rabaul	4 Zeros
12, 13	26 Dec 43	Cape Gloucester	2 Zeros
14, 15	30 Mar 44	Hollandia	2 Oscars
16	31 Mar 44	Hollandia	1 Oscar
17, 18	12 Apr 44	Hollandia	2 Tonys
19, 20	16 Jun 44	Owi Island	2 Zeros
21	17 Aug 44	Amboina Is.	1 Oscar
22	6 Nov 44	Mindanao	1 Oscar

Thomas Joseph Lynch

Tommy Lynch was one of the most natural fighter pilots to serve in the Fifth Air Force. He was highly regarded by other members of the 39th Fighter Squadron with which he flew from its first combat days in the spring of 1942. One example of the confidence others had in Lynch was the mission of May 8, 1943. Lynch had turned the squadron over to his deputy because of a malfunction in his drop tank and was preparing to short the mission when he noticed the rest of the squadron following his lead. He resumed the mission and even accounted for an enemy fighter—the only one scored by the 39th that month.

Lynch assumed command of the 39th on March 24, 1943, after the former commander was assigned to lead the 475th Fighter Group. After a break in his Pacific tour from September 1943 until the beginning of 1944, Lynch began his freelance missions with Dick Bong. The last combat report he made is indicative of Lynch's mettle in action:

> . . . On the return flight (from Wewak) I sighted 5 Oscars flying towards DAGUA from the direction of WEWAK at about 3,000 feet. I was then at 17,000 feet. I dropped my tanks and made a tail attack on the rear plane in the enemy formation. The OSCAR burst into flames and fell of flaming from my first burst. I made several more passes with nil results and then sighted 6 more enemy aircraft approaching. We started to return to base and then decided to attack again. I made a headon pass at an OSCAR and observed hits around the engine. A fairly large piece of metal came off his plane and hit behind my left prop, denting the engine cowling. I made two more passes and then called to captain BONG to break off.

Lynch by P-38G-1 s/n 42-12715 of the 39th Fighter Squadron.

Thomas Joseph Lynch Victory List

No.	Date	Jap. Aircraft	Remark
1-2	20 May 42	2 Zeros	Scored in P-400
3	26 May 42	Zero	Scored in P-400
Lynch shot down and injured on 16 June 42.			
4-5	27 Dec 42	2 Oscars	Lynch became ace
6-7	31 Dec 42	2 Zeros	
8	8 Jan 43	Oscar	5th P-38 victory.
9	3 Mar 43	Zero	
10	8 May 43	Zero	Lynch pursued attack with hung drop-tank
11	10 Jun 43	Dinah	Only victory scored by 39th in June 43
12-13	20 Aug 43	2 Twin-engine fighters	
14	21 Aug 43	Oscar	
15	4 Sep 43	Dive-bomber	
16	16 Sep 43	Dinah	Lynch transferred to V Fighter Command
17	10 Feb 44	Lily	
18-19	3 Mar 44	2 Tonys	
20	5 Mar 44	Oscar	

Portrait of Tom Lynch in New Guinea.   USAF

Daniel Tipton Roberts

Roberts was the commander of the 433rd Fighter Squadron from October 3 to November 9, 1943, the day that he was killed in action. During that time his unit was credited with fifty-five confirmed aerial victories for the loss of three pilots. There were at least ten days of perfect maintenance when not a single aircraft aborted a mission. During that period Roberts himself accounted for eight Japanese aircraft including five over the hotly contested Rabaul area. Whenever the great leaders of V Fighter Command are mentioned, Danny Roberts' name is prominently listed.

Born in Tucumcari, New Mexico, he spent his early life on a ranch near Raton and nurtured a healthy love of the out-of-doors. He went to college at Las Vegas, New Mexico, and studied music—hardly the sort of discipline that would presage a great fighter pilot. But, Roberts loved music and choral work and taught the subject to public school students in Des Moines, New Mexico, until he entered pilot training in 1941. He went through primary at San Diego, basic at Randolph and advanced at Brooks. Assigned to the 80th Fighter Squadron of the 8th Fighter Group, he was on his way to New Guinea within a week after Pearl Harbor.

Stranded in Australia while he served as commander of an air base in the middle of the desert, Roberts languished until somebody with influence took pity on his plight and sent him back to the 80th at Port Moresby. He arrived on July 21, 1942, and the next day was in a flight of P-39s trying to stop the Japanese landing at Buna. Roberts' flight strafed the landing ground but the leader of the flight was shot down. Roberts was scared stiff when he realized that he had not even looked at a map of New Guinea and had no idea of where he was flying. Fortunately, he was able to dead reckon home.

He was able to score against Japanese aircraft for the first time on August 26, during another raid on Buna. This time the P-39 leader was the one who was lost and led the flight in the wrong direction to Milne Bay. Roberts diplomatically broke radio silence and suggested that they had a better chance of finding the enemy by crossing the Owen Stanley Mountains. Their course was changed abruptly and the flight had one of the 80th Fighter Squadron's best days with the P-39 when they caught the Japanese just as their planes were taking off. Six Zeros were claimed including two for Roberts.

Two more victories were to fall to Danny Roberts while he served with the 80th. These two victories were Val dive-bombers caught around Oro Bay on April 11, 1943, for Roberts' first claims in the P-38. His first tally for the 432nd Fighter Squadron came on the day of the third big mission for the group. August 21, 1943, was also the day that he became an ace, witnessed by his combat report:

Was leading Clover flights—about three minutes from target (Dagua and But dromes) about 8 or 10 enemy planes began to attack B-25s. Radio instructions given to drop tanks—called no. 2 flight, for an attack. Enemy made overhead passes. Copper flights went ahead to target as ordered. Clover flights dropped down to give close cover. Several passes made from about 6,500 ft. One (Hamp) left smoking badly. My wingman, Lt. Michener, possibly got some bursts in here also.

Radio call supposedly came from B-25s saying, "Zeros over target." Lt. Michener and I went alone to target area, balance of squadron was heavily engaged. Twenty to twenty-five enemy planes seen from three to eight thousand feet. One P-38 in trouble with 6 "Haps" (Hamps)*. A forward rush to help him was in vain, just before we got in range he, the P-38, rolled over, smoked slightly and went straight in, in flames.

I took the second "Hap" who followed our P-38, he was slightly above and behind. My fire entered his nose section. He exposed his belly and "went in" near the But strip, after smoking violently. A previous burst into a "Hap" proved successful when he attempted to continue climbing, fell off and crashed into the sea off the Dagua strip.

Lt. Michener and I left the strip at full throttle from about 3,000 ft, were pursued by about 8 enemy aircraft which followed for approximately two minutes. On passing the WEWAK and BORAM areas about 8 or 10 P-38s were observed with 3 or 4 enemy planes at about 10,000 feet. An attempted radio rendezvous with B-25s at Karau lagoon was unsuccessful. One "copper" plane from 80th Squadron followed us to the Markham Valley.

Lt. Michener and I flew on to 30 MILE for fuel because the weather was getting worse in the Marilinan area.

I claim two "Haps" destroyed.

Danny Roberts photographed by Dennis Cooper.

One mission that was particularly successful for the 433rd after Roberts took command was flown on October 17, 1943, the day that McGuire and several other 475th pilots were handled roughly by the Japanese. The 433rd, however, claimed ten without a loss. Roberts must have been shocked by his two victories when one Japanese pilot jumped without benefit of a parachute and another burned to death in his cockpit only a few feet from his victor's eyes.

Whatever may have happened to the record of the 433rd had Roberts lived is only speculation, of course, but his influence was undeniable. The crucible of war had ironically magnified the talents of the music teacher from New Mexico, then extinguished them.

Generals Whitehead and Wurtsmith contributing to the delinquency of an ace.   AFM

Probably the P-38G used by Bong during his combat of July 28, 1943. That fighter was damaged and taken out of service after Bong's mission.

Cpl. W. Finkel, Barden and Bong after 21st victory. s/n 42-66847.   Elwood Barden

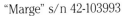

"Marge" s/n 42-103993

Chapter 11

P-38 Ace Mounts

1. *DICK BONG* Bong's first victory was scored in John Lane's #15 "Thumper." Since Bong did not stay with the 39th for more than a few weeks, he probably did not have a regularly assigned aircraft. His regularly assigned P-38 for the early days with the 9th Squadron is unknown but he did fly #73 when he scored his victory over an Oscar on July 28, 1943. The first known P-38 to carry Bong's name as pilot was #79. This aircraft was adorned with twenty-one victory flags.

By the time Bong began his second tour he had started his relationship with Marge Vattendahl and named subsequent P-38s "Marge." The first was lost in March 1944 when another pilot was flying it cross-country and bailed out after experiencing mechanical trouble in bad weather. Another was lost under similar circumstances when another pilot had to abort a takeoff in November, 1944. The dark rectangular patch on the P-38 marked with 27 victories is the place where Marge's picture was positioned before it tore away in flight in April 1944. Incidently, Marge's picture was tinted to show flesh tones and highlights.

42-104380 with temporary reapplication of Marge's portrait (#938 on tail).

P-38J-15 s/n 42-103993 "Marge."

Steve Chuboy

"Marge" used for publicity purposes. P-38J-20 s/n 44-23481.

2. *TOM MCGUIRE* McGuire also named his P-38s after his wife. The first "Pudgy" lasted only a short time and the second served McGuire throughout the rest of 1943. (He was shot down on October 17 in Frank Nichols' #110. In spite of his wounds, McGuire was worried that Nichols would be upset about the loss of his airplane!) Pudgy III saw McGuire through most of the battles during the first half of 1944 but it is most likely that he went to the Philippines in Pudgy IV. He was using another P-38 when he was killed on January 7, 1945. (Fred Champlin's #112 was reportedly the P-38 lost with McGuire. Pudgy V had already been used up in combat and McGuire was waiting for his new P-38, which would presumably have become Pudgy VI.) All markings were scraped from Pudgy V and it subsequently disappeared to some other unit's roster.

"Pudgy III" AFM

"Pudgy V" Frank Kish

"Pudgy II" P-38H-5 s/n 42-66817

"Pudgy IV"

3. *COLONEL MACDONALD* Like Bong, Charles Mac-Donald used a borrowed Lightning to score his first victory. MacDonald had commanded the 340th Fighter Squadron, flying P-47s before he came over to Headquarters, 475th Fighter Group. He managed to pilfer P-38 #193 from the 433rd Squadron on October 15, 1943, and intercepted the formation of Vals, downing two of them.

The first Putt-Putt Maru was a P-47. The first P-38 Putt-Putt Maru was an olive drab camouflaged P-38H. The second was a natural metal P-38, which he flew during the early part of 1944. The third was a P-38L, which must have been brought to the Pacific no earlier than July 1944. (The AAF serial was 44-24843.) MacDonald had the third P-38 on Leyte and used two subsequent L-models before he went home in the spring of 1945.

2nd P-P-M

5th P-P-M P-38L-5 s/n 44-25471

3rd P-P-M P-38L-1 s/n 44-24843

4. *GERALD JOHNSON* Johnson used aircraft numbered #83 until he assumed command of the 49th Fighter Group. There is no clear indication of special markings prior to his assuming command aside from the hint of a drawing on photo on page 18. Later P-38s that he flew, however, were named "Barbara" for his wife and "Jerry" for himself. He sometimes flew his later P-38 with a victory marking for the Australian aircraft that he accidently shot down. (Wirraway or Boomerang?) That particular vanity was probably a bit indiscreet and undoubtedly caused some requests in embarrassed quarters for its removal. Another interesting marking is the faint circle that appears on some of Johnson's later aircraft photos. There is an image barely visible in the center and may have been some effort by Johnson to portray his wife on the aircraft in the fashion of Dick Bong's "Marge."

4th P-P-M P-38L-5 s/n 44-25643

Johnson's P-47D. Airplane had white ailerons.

Johnson's P-38 on Biak.

Carl Bong

Bob DeHaven

Johnson by his P-38 "Barbara" early summer 1945.

Aschenbrener

5. *JAY T. ROBBINS* Contrary to popular notion, Robbins did not name all his P-38s "Jandina," per the photos displayed elsewhere. It was probably "Jandina III" that was pranged on the Saidor strip. It was certainly made airworthy again since evidence indicates that Robbins flew it thereafter. Note that Robbins had command stripes at least sometime during the life of Jandina III and that he flew aircraft letter "A" at one time.

2nd Jandina

"Jandina III"

"Jandina IV"

6. *ET AL* Ed Cragg flew a nice looking P-38 and it is probably this one that he used on his last mission. Similarly, Ken Ladd flew several interesting P-38s and he probably went down in #7. There are few good photos of George Welch's P-38 and this one was included in the group purely out of frustration. Joel Paris' P-38 was included to help correct some misconceptions about his aircraft decorations and Wallace Jordan's P-38 was included because it is strikingly simple and uncluttered. Harry Sealy represents the CBI side and this picture should correct some mistakes about his markings. Although this is an earlier model than usually represented, note that the number on the tail is 121 *not* 12. Also, there has never been much evidence for those gaudy green flourishes that have made the rounds. Finally, the P-38 of Obie Taylor is a nice representative of 14th Fighter Group P-38s. The entire aircraft is natural metal with olive drab anti-glare panels and blue spinners. Other markings are in black and the swastikas are in the standard style for the P-38s of the 14th Fighter Group. The group emblem is displayed on the left engine cowling and is white (representing silver) and dark blue. The motto beneath is "To fight to Death."

Full shot of Maj. Ed Cragg's "Porky II" in August 1943.

P-38J-20-Lo s/n 44-23301, probably Ladd's last P-38 (wheel and spokes: Black, Steel Blue outlined Black; Speed marks: Steel Blue; Tear Drops: Steel blue outlined Black). Crew chief: S/Sgt A.K. Saidey.

Ken Ladd by "Windy City Ruthie." Note white slippage marks on nose wheel.

Joel Paris by his P-38L-5 s/n 44-25453. Georgia: medium blue, Belle: black, Martha: black, Marjorie: black. Left bot. shadow: yellow.   Krane

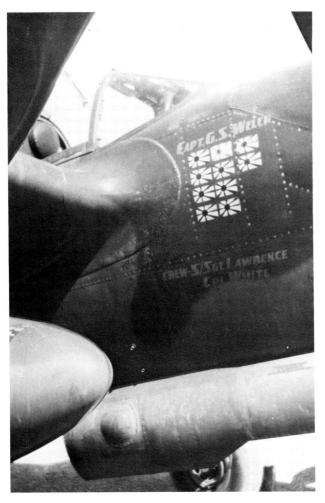

Closeup of Welch's scoreboard. Krane

Victory marks on Wallace Jordan's P-38L. Jordan

Harry Sealy's first "Haleakala" (Hawaiian phrase meaning "House of the Sun"). U.S. Army

Fifth Air Force P-38s assigned to aces circa September 1, 1943

39th Fighter Squadron
10. Tom Lynch
15. John Lane
22. Stanley Andrews
23. Charles Sullivan
26. Richard Smith
27. Charles King
30. Paul Stanch

9th Fighter Squadron
70. Ralph Wire
79. Dick Bong
83. Gerald Johnson
84. James Watkins
91. Wallace Jordan
96. Ralph Wandrey
99. John O'Neill

80th Fighter Squadron
A. Ed Cragg
E. George Welch
H. Allen Hill
J. Jay Robbins
M. Louis Schriber
V. Cyril Homer
X. Paul Murphey

431st Fighter Squadron
111. Vincent Elliot
117. Paul Morriss
118. Harry Brown
120. Verl Jett
121. Frank Monk
124. Fred Champlin
125. Marion Kirby
131. Tom McGuire
134. Francis Lent

432nd Fighter Squadron
143. Elliott Summer
144. James Ince
146. Zach Dean
147. Henry Condon
161. John Loisel
168. Billy Gresham

433rd Fighter Squadron
179. Joseph McKeon
191. Jack Fisk

5AF

Aircraft of P-38 aces lost in action and aircraft in which P-38 aces were downed.

March 3, 1943 (F-5) 42-12633 Hoyt A. Eason
Sept. 22, 1943 (H-1) 42-66579 Vivian Cloud
Oct. 17, 1943 (H-1) 42-66836
Jan. 7, 1945 (L-1) 44-24845 Tom McGuire
Dec. 26, 1943 (H-1) 42-66506 Ed Cragg
Mar. 24, 1944 (J-15) 42-103993
Nov. 28, 1944 (L-) — Dick Bong
Nov. 9, 1943 (H-1) 42-66546 Danny Roberts
Nov. 10, 1944 (L-1) 44-23957 Perry Dahl
Dec. 7, 1944 (L-1) 44-23945 Meryl Smith
Jan. 15, 1945 (L-1) 44-25336 Paul Lucas
8AF
March 18, 1944 (J-10) 42-69726 Lindol F. Graham
Code letters: MC-L

Oliver Taylor taxiing in "PAT III."   Taylor

Some of the old P-38 pilots were in the P-80 program at the end of the war. Seventh from right, standing: Maj. Robin Olds; Leon Gray was leading F-5 recon pilot, kneeling second from left; Meldrum Sears is kneeling fifth from left and Rex Barber is on his left. Bruce Holloway, SAC chief in the '60s and CBI ace is on the right of Sears and John Herbst, top ace of the CBI is kneeling at the right end.

USAF

Chapter 12
About the Pilots

*D*URING MAY 1975 ABOUT ONE HUN-dred P-38 veterans met at the Registry Hotel in Minneapolis, Minnesota for the first such reunion of ex-Lightning pilots. I had the pleasure of contacting many of the pilots who had contributed much of the background of the P-38 ace research. It was with a decided eagerness that I drove to the stately looking hotel near the Minneapolis-St. Paul International Airport.

One of the first people I saw in the darkened lobby was my old friend Carl Bong, dead ringer for his brother Dick and generous researcher in anything having to do with the P-38. I believe it was Carl who suggested that David Tallichet's P-38 was coming soon and that we should hustle across the road to the airport. As wide-eyed as I probably was at the prospect of finding all the veterans and aces standing in the corridors of the hotel, I didn't want to miss the arrival of the glorious P-38 painted in the colors of the 20th Fighter Group.

And indeed it was an experience. One of the people standing by the fightline waiting to welcome Tallichet was Art Heiden. I eagerly accepted the opportunity to meet face-to-face the person who had provided those accounts of Lindol Graham. We were able to talk for a few minutes and Art's disarming manner took over and he told several stories of the fascinating 20th Fighter Group and his awe at being the young wingman of a great P-38 pilot like Graham.

Someone announced the arrival of Tallichet's P-38 and we all looked to the western sky and saw the unmistakable shape sweeping toward us. With a theatrical flourish Tallichet banked the glistening Lightning toward starboard and we got a good look at the sleek plan of the unique airplane before it was turned on final approach. Within a few minutes it was taxiing before us like a prima donna, its 20th Fighter Group markings as prominent as all the world. I bet Art that the sight brought back memories and one glance in his direction told me that I had won.

But we all got our chance to climb the venerable P-38's ladder and sit in the cockpit. I satisfied myself that the critics of the supposed cramped cockpit were filled with unspeakable nonsense and that the view was as good as any other fighter that I had experienced, including the P-51D. However, since the only airplane that I had flown myself was the diminutive Cessna 150, my status was that of novice.

Nevertheless, the view was unobstructed from every quarter save the ten and two o'clock positions partially covered by the engines. Rear vision was remarkably unobstructed although Tallichet's airplane did not have the bulky armor plate or old signal corps radio installed. In any event, an alert Lightning pilot should not have had any problem avoiding surprises from stalking enemy fighters.

Anyway, it was time to meet some of the aces who had flown the P-38. It was with some natural—or perhaps unnatural—reluctance that I went with Art back to the hotel. Some of the members of the International Plastic Modeler's Society were there in a giant sunken fireplace pit that graced one end of the hotel lobby. My old friends Ken Ring and Jack Mugan were holding forth once again and I joined them in one of the unbelievably deep and comfortable easy chairs that mark the Registry as a bastion of civilization.

Part of the reason we were able to get this particular reunion together was the support of the Midwest portion, or Region 5, of the IPMS. For the sake of this convention Region 5 went P-38 crazy and brought enough models along to do a proper job of duplicating the entire P-38 fleet at any one point in the Lockheed's career. I was honored by the request that I be one of the judges in the P-38 contest. As it turned out, I made the faux pas of selecting every P-38 model in that portion of the contest for a prize except Jack Mugan's. The models were anonymous and when I found out that Jack had built the impressive-looking P-38M that had been snubbed for no good reason, I mentally kicked myself.

But, before I digress further, let me go on to the P-38 pilots that I met. One of the first people that I ran into (actually, I think Ken Ring surreptitiously ferreted these P-38 aces out and got me pointed in their direction; it was part of Ken's public relations genius) was Tom Maloney. And what a gentle person Tom was. I was glad to find that his ordeal in southern France had not left any apparent permanent damage on him. The last time any of his friends had seen him in the French hospital they were not certain that he would survive, let alone fully recover. Whether or

Gerald Brown and friend with Don and Sylvia Penn during happier times at Los Angeles Coconut Grove after the war.   Penn

not his experience had mellowed him, Maloney was surprisingly soft-spoken and mild in nature considering his wartime record.

I happened to be with Art Heiden when he met Col. Charles King. King was another friendly and warm personality who seemed unlikely to have been in all the rough action he endured. I was getting to like this new experience a great deal when King talked expansively on the exploits of Tom Lynch and Dick Bong and all the others we had read about in the 39th Fighter Squadron. Wonder of wonders, King even agreed to help as much as possible when I suggested that it would be interesting to do a history of the 39th. And help he did, with a packet of documents and photographs practically once a week for the next six months!

On the last night of the reunion we all showed up for the banquet. I even had the audacity to make an appearance in a trainer-yellow leisure suit. Of course, I was introduced during the dinner and had to stand up like a giant canary. But enough of mea culpa; I felt that I was among friends and that anything was forgivable.

After the dinner, Art Heiden introduced me to Dick Suehr who was sitting at Carl Bong's table. I was especially eager to meet Suehr since he was right there when Dick Bong claimed his fifth victory. At that particular time I wanted desperately to determine Bong's confirmed victories and this was a rare chance to talk to an eyewitness. Things did not go well with Suehr, however, and all I managed to learn from him was that he thought the P-38 was an excellent escort fighter. So be it. The reunion was his and he was deep in nostalgia and I didn't want to interfere with it all.

Ralph Wandrey was a different matter. I had been looking for Ralph all during the reunion and managed to find him just as the banquet was breaking up. Ralph was another pleasant person to know. With a quick sense of humor and absolutely keen mind to draw from, he was a joy to listen to. We spent the rest of the evening and the early hours of the next morning talking about the war—the Pacific air war and New Guinea in specific.

Ralph told unabashedly how he earned the name "Ironass" by threatening to court-martial any wingman who lost him in combat. He was solidly convinced that most fatalities in air battles were alone when they died. Wandrey therefore wanted every P-38 pilot in the 9th Fighter Squadron to be very chummy and have plenty of company around—or else.

Wandrey also told the story of Jerry Johnson coming to him just before the Rabaul operations and asking him to say something to a glum bunch of 9th Squadron pilots. Wandrey got up during the briefing for the first Rabaul mission and told the new pilots, especially, how the Japanese had been having their own way up to that moment. He told how the Allies had been taking it on the defensive while the Japanese called the shots from the relatively safe haven at Rabaul. Now was the time for swift retribution and a positive offensive strike at Japanese air power.

Whether or not he was effective in his little pep talk Ralph could not say for certain. However, it is a fact that the 9th Squadron earned a Distinguished Unit Citation for claiming twenty-four Japanese fighters over Rabaul. It is also a fact that only two P-38s from the squadron were reported missing during the month-long Fifth Air Force campaign over the area.

As it was, the talk I had with Wandrey was the fitting climax to a memorable meeting with these P-38 veterans.

Calvin Wire, Jack Purdy and Bill Grady of the 433rd F.S. and "Red" Herman of the 431st at a 475th Fighter Group reunion in the '60s.   Krane

Dick Suehr and Ralph Wandrey meet at the first P-38 pilot's convention, May 1975 in Minneapolis.

Twin Cities Aero Historians

Art Heiden is living in Tennessee now and enjoys occasional flings at aviation during his semi-retirement. Colonel King is retired from the Air Force and lives a pleasant existence by a lake in rural Wisconsin. Ralph Wandrey was medically retired from the Army and had a touch-and-go bout with several diseases before he prevailed, as may be expected from an old "hardass." Ralph is now living in Arizona.

Tom Maloney is living in Oklahoma and was on the verge of retirement when I last heard from him. Dick Suehr is living in North Carolina. The fate of the other P-38 pilots made me wonder how I could track them down and to some extent I was successful.

Of course, there are those who survived the war only to fall victim to peacetime attrition. Jerry Johnson is a prime example. He loved to take risks and flew through some questionable weather over Japan in October, 1945. That he didn't make it is attributable to the daredevil Johnson rather than the supreme combat leader who forged such wickedly effective formations under his command.

George Welch is another example. He was test-flying an F-100 on an October day in 1954 when the thing stalled on landing and Welch was too low for an effective bail out. One of his squadronmates, Cy Homer, attended an 80th Squadron reunion a few years ago and was feeling well when he returned home. Yet, within a short time he fell ill and died.

But many of the P-38 aces are still alive and well. Charles MacDonald had a frustrating career in the Air Force. Apparently he continued with the same aloofness that he practiced in command of the 475th. With few friends in the right places, it is possible that MacDonald was frustrated with his prospects of becoming a general and left the service at the earliest possible moment. He retired in 1961 and reportedly took a cruise around the world. He still resists attempts to intrude into his private world and at last report was living somewhere in Costa Rica.

The first and last P-38 aces of World War II are living worlds apart. Jack Ilfrey has written a book of his experiences in World War II and is as irrepressible as ever living in San Antonio. I met Jack face-to-face at an Eighth Air Force convention in St. Paul in 1981. In Jack's case the old rascal fighter pilot is still there and it is not hard to imagine a young Jack Ilfrey flying his P-38 out of internment or being broken in rank for stealing the operations jeep. George Laven is still involved with military aviation in Israel as a representative of the McDonnell-Douglas Company. Considering the 60-1 edge the Israeli pilots racked up early in 1982, George must be doing a good job.

As for the others, they seem to be grouping themselves geographically. In California we have reports of Bob Buttke of the 55th Fighter Group. Calvin Wire, Vincent Elliott and Verl Jett are among the 475th veterans living in California. Tom Lanphier and John Mitchell also returned to California, Lanphier from an airline career and Mitchell from the Air Force.

Besides Ilfrey in Texas there is also his squadronmate, the current Dr. Newell Roberts. "Duckbutt" Watkins, "Jack" Jones and John Loisel are representatives of the Fifth Air Force who retired to the Lone Star State and Col. Harley Vaughn also settled in Texas after he retired.

Florida claims several old P-38 aces. James Morris of the 20th Group lives there as does John Tilley, another old 475th hand. Two old veterans of the 14th Fighter Group, Jack Lenox and Bill Leverette live in Florida while their former commander was one of those who migrated to California. "Obie" Taylor now lives in Sausalito and helps struggling young writers when he can.

Two old Eighth Air Force tigers live in Colorado. Robin Olds lives relatively close to John Lowell in the magnificent and rugged country of the Rockies. Jerry Brown lives in no less beautiful country. Twice made a prisoner-of-war, once by the Germans and once by the Koreans, Brown lives in Arizona. Another 475th pilot, Joe Forster, lives nearby in another part of Arizona.

Other pilots seem to have vanished completely. Bill Harris probably retired from the Air Force as a colonel and returned to California. "Dixie" Sloan is now retired in Ohio but prefers to remain relatively incommunicado. Michael Brezas was the other great P-38 pilot in the Mediterranean and, of course, was lost in Korea.

General Vandenberg and John Mitchell during the Korean War. Mitchell claimed 4 MiGs during the Korean tour.   USAF

Tom Maloney at far right and (l-r) Jack Loveless, Harold Lindquist and John Price—all pilots of the 1st Fighter Group at the P-38 pilot's convention, Minneapolis, Minnesota 1975.   TCAH

Appendix

COMMANDER AIR
SOLOMON ISLANDS
U.S. SOUTH PACIFIC FORCE

May 30, 1943

MEMORANDUM FOR:
Commander Aircraft South Pacific Force.

Subject:
Investigation concerning leakage of information concerning the fighter sweep of the Kihili area on April 18, 1943.

1. Upon receipt of informaton that an important Japanese naval officer was flying into the Kihili-Ballale area about 1000 Love, April 18th, a conference was held in the Admiral's cabin with the Admiral, General Harris and Commander Ring present. These two officers were told the contents of the dispatch just received and all present agreed that a conference should be held immediately with Fighter Command representatives to discuss possible means of interception.

2. This conference was held later in the morning, again in the Admiral's office. Present were: General F. Harris, USMC, Chief of Staff; Commander S. C. Ring, USN, Ass't Chief of Staff for Operations; Commander W. A. Read, USNR, Ass't Chief of Staff for Administration; Lt. Col. E. L. Pugh, USMC, Fighter Command OIC; Lt. Col. H. Viccellio, AAF, Fighter Command Ass't OIC; Major J. P. Condon, USMC, Fighter Commands Operations Officer; Major J. W. Mitchell, AAF, Proposed Strike Group Commander; Capt. T. G. Lanphier, AAF, Attack Section Leader of Strike Group.

3. All present were informed of the fact that a MOST SECRET dispatch had been received concerning the flight of an important Japanese naval officer into the Kihili area the following day and asked for comments on possible means of interception. It was obvious from the beginning of the discussion that all officers present considered the mission a most hazardous one and the chances of interception very slight indeed. In order to impress all concerned with the importance of a successful interception and to provide an additional incentive for the flight, disclosure was made of the Japanese naval officer involved. No mention whatsoever was made of the source of information contained in the dispatch. A plan was formulated and presented by General Harris to Admiral Mitscher who approved it in the presence of Admiral Fitch.

4. Upon completion of the conference in the Admiral's cabin the Fighter Command representatives adjourned to the Fighter Command dug-out where the mechanics of the strike were laid out. Present were:
Lt. Col. E. L. Pugh, USMC
*Lt. Col. L. S. Moore, USMC, Fighter Command Ass't OIC
Lt. Col. H. Viccellio, AAF
Major J. P. Condon, USMC
Major J. W. Mitchell, AAF
Capt. T. G. Lanphier, AAF
*Lt. P. Lewis, (A-V(S)), USNR, Fighter Command Intelligence Officer
(*Additional officers informed of the particulars of the strike)

Plans were laid out concerning course, speed and altitude to the Kihili area, point of anticipated interception, and return flight to Henderson. The discussion took place around the map table of the dug-out and no other people were present.

5. Later in the evening a conference was held in Major Mitchell's tent of all the pilots who were to take part in the following day's operations. Present were:
Attacking Section: Capt. T. G. Lanphier, AAF
1st Lt. R. T. Barber, AAF
1st Lt. B. T. Holmes, AAF
1st Lt. H. K. Hine, AAF

Covering Section: Major J. W. Mitchell, AAF
Major L. R. Kittel, AAF
1st Lt. J. Jacobson, AAF
1st Lt. D. S. Canning, AAF
1st Lt. D. C. Georke, AAF

1st Lt. R. J. Ames, AAF
1st Lt. L. A. Graebner, AAF
1st Lt. E. H. Anglin, AAF
1st Lt. W. E. Smith, AAF
1st Lt. A. R. Long, AAF
1st Lt. E. E. Stratton, AAF
2nd Lt. G. Whittiker, AAF

In addition to the pilots above, Lt. (jg) J. E. McGuigan, A-V(S), USNR, Air Combat Intelligence Officer, was present to brief the pilots on location of friendly coastwatchers and natives. Admiral Yamamoto's name was mentioned in this conference.

The following morning the strike group took off on schedule and made a successful interception. The officers returning were briefed in a routine manner with only Lt. Col. E. L. Pugh, USMC, Lt. Col. H. Viccellio, AAF, Major J. P. Condon, USMC, and Capt. W. Morrison, AAF, a USAF-ISPA representative, present. According to Capt. Morrison, the only reference made concerning the enemy naval officer concerned was a remark, believed to have come from Capt. Lanphier, that, "That son of a bitch won't dictate any peace terms in the White House."

6. In accordance with instructions from Headquarters, Air Command, the action report was prepared and submitted treating the strike as a routine fighter sweep.

7. No evidence has been unearthed which would indicate that any information concerning this strike was passed to newspapermen directly or indirectly.

M. A. MITSCHER

P-38 ACE LIST

The names included on this list are those P-38 pilots with five or more confirmed victories. Final tabulations were made from individual or unit records and should be accurate within one or two victories.

Fifth Air Force

Name	P-38 Score	Total WWII	Major Units
Richard I. Bong	40	40	HQ V Fighter Command
Thomas B. McGuire	38	38	431st F.S.
Charles H. MacDonald	27	27	HQ 475th F.G.
Jay T. Robbins	22	22	80th F.S.
Gerald R. Johnson	20	22-24	HQ 49 F.G.
Thomas J. Lynch	17	20	39th F.S.
Edward Cragg	15	15	80th F.S.
Cyril F. Homer	15	15	80th F.S.
Daniel T. Roberts	13	15	433rd F.S.
Kenneth G. Ladd	12	12	80th F.S.
Francis J. Lent	11	11	431st F.S.
John S. Loisel	11	11	432nd F.S.
Cornelius Smith	11	11	80th F.S.
Kenneth Sparks	11	11	39th F.S.
James A. Watkins	11	12	9th F.S.
William Giroux	10	10	36th F.S.
Paul Stanch	10	10	39th F.S.
Elliott Summer	10	10	432nd F.S.
Frederic F. Champlin	9	9	431st F.S.
Perry J. Dahl	9	9	432nd F.S.
Grover E. Fanning	9	9	9th F.S.
Joseph M. Forster	9	9	432nd F.S.
Allen Hill	9	9	80th F.S.
Meryl M.D Smith	9	9	HQ 475th F.G.
Fernley Damstrom	8	8	8th F.S.
Robert W. Aschenbrener	8	10	8th F.S.
Frederick Harris	8	8	432nd F.S.
Kenneth Hart	8	8	433rd F.S.
John G. O'Neill	8	8	9th F.S.
George Welch	8	16	80th F.S.
Richard West	8	12-14	35th F.S.
Burnell Adams	7	8	80th F.S.
Zach W. Dean	7	7	432nd F.S.
John S. Dunaway	7	7	36th F.S.
Vincent T. Elliot	7	7	431st F.S.
Jack A. Fisk	7	7	433rd F.S.
Warren R. Lewis	7	7	433rd F.S.
John Purdy	7	7	433rd F.S.
Richard E. Smith	7	7	39th F.S.
Calvin Wire	7	7	433rd F.S.
David W. Allen	6	8	431st F.S.
Stanley O. Andrews	6	6	39th F.S.
Edward J. Czarnecki	6	6	431st F.S.
Edwin DeGraffenreid	6	6	80th F.S.
William C. Drier	6	6	8th F.S.
Hoyt Eason	6	6	39th F.S.
Charles Gallup	6	6	39th F.S.
Billy Gresham	6	6	432nd F.S.
James Ince	6	6	432nd F.S.
Verle Jett	6	7	431st F.S.
John Lane	6	6	39th F.S.
Paul Lucas	6	6	432nd F.S.
Paul Murphey, Jr.	6	6	80th F.S.
John Pietz	6	6	431st F.S.
Horace Reeves	6	6	431st F.S.
Louis Schriber	6	6	80th F.S.
Robert Adams	5	5	80th F.S.
Ernest Ambort	5	5	9th F.S.
Harry Brown	5	7	431st F.S.
Nial Castle	5	5	8th F.S.
Vivian Cloud	5	5	432nd F.S.
Henry Condon	5	5	432nd F.S.
Warren Curton	5	5	9th F.S.
Cheatham W. Gupton	5	5	9th F.S.
Wallace Jordan	5	6	9th F.S.
Marion Kirby	5	5	431st F.S.
Charles King	5	5	39th F.S.
George Laven	5	5	HQ 49th F.G.

Name	P-38 Score	Total WWII	Unit
Alfred Lewelling*	5	5	9th F.S.
Lowell Lutton	5	5	431st F.S.
Jack Mankin	5	5	431st F.S.
Milden Mathre	5	5	7th F.S.
Franklin Monk	5	5	431st F.S.
Paul Morris	5	5	431st F.S.
Leslie Nelson*	5	5	9th F.S.
Joel Paris	5	9	8th F.S.
Jennings Myers	5	5	80th F.S.
Charles Ray	5	5	80th F.S.
John Smith	5	6	433rd F.S.
John Tilley	5	5	431st F.S.
Ralph Wandrey	5	6	9th F.S.
Arthur Wenige	5	6	431st F.S.
Ralph Wire	5	5	9th F.S.

*These 9th Fighter Squadron pilots are sometimes listed with only four victories. There is some evidence for each of them to be listed as P-38 aces. Another case is that of William Haney. However, no documents seem to justify Haney's inclusion at present.

The following pilots are credited with four victories while flying the P-38 and may have scored the requisite fifth victory for inclusion on the list.

Robert DeHaven
Jess Gidley
Richard Suehr
James W. Harris
Curran Jones
Don Hanover
Sammy Pierce
Kenneth Pool
Charles Sullivan

Thirteenth Air Force

Name	P-38 Score	Total WWII	Major Units
Bill Harris	16	16	347 F.G.
Robert B. Westbrook	13	20	18/347
Murray Shubin	11	11	18
Cotesworth Head	8	12	18
Thomas Walker	6	6	347
Rex Barber	5	5	347
George T. Chandler	5	5	347
Besby Holmes	5	5	347
Thomas Lanphier	5	5	347
Henry Meigs II	5	6	6 NFS/339 Sq
John W. Mitchell	5	11	347
Truman Barnes	5	5	347

CBI

The following pilots were credited by their various headquarters with the listed victories.

449th Squadron
Lee O. Gregg 7

Keith Mahon 5
Samuel Palmer 5
Robert Schultz (Changed to Shoals after WWII) 5

459th Squadron
Walter F. Duke 13
Hampton Boggs 9
Maxwell Glenn 7.5
Aaron Bearden 5
Burdette Goodrich 5
Harry Sealey 5
Willard Webb 5

Twelfth and Fifteenth Air Forces

Name	P-38 Score	Unit and Air Force
Michael Brezas	12	14 F.G. 15
William J. Sloan	12	82 F.G. 12
William L. Leverette	11	14 F.G. 15
Frank D. Hurlbut	9	82 F.G. 12
Louis E. Curdes	8	82 F.G. 12
Walter J. Carroll	8	82 F.G. 15
Thomas E. Maloney	8	1 F.G. 15
Claude R. Kinsey	7	82 F.G. 12
Ward A. Kuentzel	7	82 F.G. 12
Lawrence Liebers	7	82 F.G. 12
Meldrum Sears	7	1 F.G. 12
Herbert E. Ross	7	14 F.G. 12
Phillip Tovrea	7	1 F.G. 15
Harley C. Vaughn	7	82 F.G. 12
Edward T. Waters	7	82 F.G. 12
Charles E. Adams, Jr.	6	82 F.G. 15
Richard A. Campbell	6	14 F.G. 12
Ray Crawford	6	82 F.G. 12
James W. Griffiss	6	1 F.G. 12
James D. Holloway	6	82 F.G. 15
Jack M. Ilfrey	6	1 F.G. 12
Donald Kienholz	6	1 F.G. 15
Armour C. Miller	6	1 F.G. 15
William J. Schildt	6	82 F.G. 12
Thomas A. White	6	82 F.G. 12
Charles J. Zubarik	6	82 F.G. 12

Name	P-38 Score	Unit and Air Force
Leslie E. Anderson	5	82 F.G. 15
Louis Benne	5	14 F.G. 15
Paul R. Cochran	5	82 F.G. 12
Rodney W. Fisher	5	1 F.G. 12
Claude E. Ford	5	82 F.G. 12
Warner F. Gardner	5	82 F.G. 12
Robert C. Griffith	5	82 F.G. 15
Harry T. Hanna	5	14 F.G. 12
Herbert Hatch	5	1 F.G. 15
Clayton M. Isaacson	5*	82 F.G. 15
Warren L. Jones	5	14 F.G. 15
Joseph Jorda	5	82 F.G. 15
Carroll S. Knott	5	14 F.G. 15

Franklin C. Lathrope	5	1 F.G.	15
Richard J. Lee	5	1 F.G.	15
Marlow Leikness	5	14 F.G.	15
Jack Lenox, Jr.	5	14 F.G.	15
John A. MacKay	5	1 F.G.	12
T. H. McArthur	5	82 F.G.	12
John W. McGuyrt	5	14 F.G.	15
Everett Miller	5	1 F.G.	15
Ernest K. Osher	5	82 F.G.	12
Joel A. Owens	5	1 F.G.	12
Newell O. Roberts	5	1 F.G.	12
Gerald Rounds	5	82 F.G.	15
Robert K. Seidman	5	14 F.G.	15
Virgil H. Smith	5	14 F.G.	12
Oliver B. Taylor	5	14 F.G.	15
Herman Visscher	5	82 F.G.	15
Darrell G. Welch	5	1 F.G.	12
Paul H. Wilkins	5	14 F.G.	15
Lee W. Wiseman	5	1 F.G.	12
John L. Wolford	5	1 F.G.	12
Max J. Wright	5	14 F.G.	15
Daniel Kennedy	5	1 F.G.	12

*One of these victories was scored with the 49th Fighter Group.

The following pilots may have scored as many as four or more victories with the P-38.

1st Fighter Group
Harold Lienau
Robert Neale
Edward Newberry
Walter Rivers

14th Fighter Group
Virgil W. Lusk
Erwin Ethel
Sidney Weatherford
Lt. Hohman
Lt. Miller
Lt. Church
Lt. White

82nd Fighter Group
Clarence O. Johnson
R. E. Kirtley

D. F. Sharp
A. K. Hamric
R. C. Leeman
M. Moore
R. P. Kinney
F. J. Wolfe
W. B. Rawson
P. O. Rodgers
J. A. Perrone

Eighth and Ninth Air Forces

Name	P-38 Score	WWII Total	Unit and Air Force
Jack M. Ilfrey	8*	8	20 F.G. 8
James Morris	7.33	7.33	20 F.G. 8
Laurence E. Blumer	6	6	367 F.G. 9
Robert Buttke	5.5	6.5	55 F.G. 8
Lindol Graham	5.5	5.5	20 F.G. 8
Gerald A. Brown	5	5	55 F.G. 8
Clarence O. Johnson	5**	7	479 F.G. 8
Lenton Kirkland	5	5	474th F.G. 9
John H. Lowell	5***	9.5	364 F.G. 8
Joseph Miller	5****	5	474 F.G. 9
Robert Milliken	5	5	474 F.G. 9
Robin Olds	5	12	479 F.G. 8

*Includes the six that Ilfrey claimed in North Africa.

**Includes at least four claimed in North Africa. Johnson was later killed in action with the 352nd Fighter Group.

***Lowell's score contains a number of probables and must therefore be qualified. There can be little doubt, however, that he claimed at least five victories with the P-38.

****Includes four scored with the 14th Fighter Group.

The following pilots may have as many as four or more victories while flying the P-38.

Arthur Jeffrey 479 F.G.
John D. Landers 55 F.G.
Joseph Griffin 367 F.G.
Chet Patterson 55 F.G.

Michael Brezas on left. Photo probably taken August 1944. Note that Virgil Smith is credited with *6* victories, giving incidental support ·to argument that he is first P-38 Ace.
Tom Collins

SCORES OF LIGHTNING ACES WITH TEN OR MORE VICTORIES

Bill Harris
(339th Fighter Squadron, 18th Fighter Group)
7 Jun 43, 2 Zeros
16 Jun 43, 2 Zeros
4 Oct 43, 1 Zero
7 Oct 43, 1 Zero
10 Oct 43, 3 Zeros
27 Oct 43, 1 Val
9 Feb 44, 3 Zeros
15 Feb 44, 2 Zeros
22 Jun 45, 1 Oscar

Bob Westbrook
(44th Fighter Squadron, 347th Fighter Group)
10 Oct 43, 1 Zero
23 Dec 43, 1 Zero
24 Dec 43, 3 Zeros
25 Dec 43, 2 Zeros
6 Jan 44, 1 Zero
25 Sep 44, 1 Oscar
30 Sep 44, 1 Oscar
23 Oct 44, 3 Oscars

William Sloan
(96th Fighter Squadron)
7 Jan 43, 1 Bf 109
30 Jan 43, 1 Bf 109
2 Feb 43, 1 Bf 109; 1 Do 217
15 Feb 43, 1 Bf 109
20 May 43, 1 Ju 88; 1 Mc 200
18 Jun 43, 1 Mc 200
5 Jul 43, 1 Re 2001; 1 Bf 109
10 Jul 43, 1 Mc 202
22 Jul 43, 1 Bf 109

Cy Homer
(80th Fighter Squadron)
21 Aug 43, 1 Tony; 2 Zeros
4 Sep 43, 1 Zero
13 Sep 43, 1 Oscar
18 Jan 44, 1 Oscar
23 Mar 44, 1 Oscar; 1 Tony
30 Mar 44, 1 Oscar
3 Apr 44, 2 Oscars, 2 Tonys
27 Jul 44, 1 Oscar
10 Nov 44, 1 Oscar

Danny Roberts
(80th Fighter Squadron, 432nd Fighter Squadron, 433rd Fighter Squadron)
11 Apr 43, 2 Vals

21 Aug 43, 2 Hamps
7 Sep 43, 1 Oscar
17 Oct 43, 2 Zeros
23 Oct 43, 2 Zeros
24 Oct 43, 1 Zero
29 Oct 43, 1 Zero
2 Nov 43, 1 Zero
9 Nov 43, 1 Hamp

Francis Lent
(431st Fighter Squadron)
18 Aug 43, 1 Hamp
21 Aug 43, 1 Nick; 1 Zero
15 Oct 43, 2 Zeros, 1 Val
24 Oct 43, 1 Tony
2 Nov 43, 1 Zero
16 Dec 43, 1 Betty
31 Mar 44, 2 Zeros

Edward Cragg
(80th Fighter Squadron)
21 May 43, 1 Hamp
21 Jul 43, 2 Zeros
23 Jul 43, 1 Tony
20 Aug 43, 1 Zero
21 Aug 43, 1 Zero; 1 Tony
4 Sept 43, 2 Zeros
24 Oct 43, 2 Zeros
29 Oct 43, 1 Zero
2 Nov 43, 1 Zero
22 Dec 43, 1 Tony
26 Dec 43, 1 Tojo

Ken Ladd
(80th Fighter Squadron, 36th Fighter Squadron)
29 Jul 43, 1 Dinah
2 Sep 43, 1 Dinah
15 Sep 43, 1 Zero
13 Dec 43, 1 Zero
17 Dec 43, 1 Zero
26 Dec 43, 2 Vals
23 Jan 44, 1 Zero
31 Mar 44, 1 Oscar
3 Apr 44, 1 Oscar
14 Oct 44, 1 Oscar; 1 Tojo

John Loisel
(432nd Fighter Squadron, 475th Fighter Group)

21 Aug 43, 2 Oscars	3 Apr 44, 2 Oscars
22 Sep 43, 1 Zero	21 Dec 43, 1 Zero
15 Oct 43, 2 Oscars	23 Jan 44, 1 Zero
13 Dec 43, 1 Zero	3 Apr 44, 2 Oscars
21 Dec 43, 1 Zero	
23 Jan 44, 1 Zero	

13 Dec 44, 1 Zero
28 Mar 45, 1 Frank

Ken Sparks
(39th Fighter Squadron)
27 Dec 42, 1 Zero; 1 Val
31 Dec 42, 2 Zeros
7 Jan 43, 1 Oscar
8 Jan 43, 2 Oscars
4 Mar 43, 1 Oscar; 1 Zero
18 Jul 43, 1 Oscar
21 Jul 43, 1 Oscar

Cornelius Smith, Jr.
(80th Fighter Squadron)
21 Jun 43, 3 Zeros
16 Oct 43, 1 Tony
24 Oct 43, 1 Zero
22 Dec 43, 1 Zero
26 Dec 43, 1 Oscar
18 Jan 44, 2 Zeros
31 Mar 44, 1 Dinah
12 Apr 44, 1 Oscar

James A. Watkins
(9th Fighter Squadron)
26 Jul 43, 4 Tonys
28 Jul 43, 3 Oscars
2 Aug 43, 3 Oscars
1 Apr 45, 1 Tojo

William K. Giroux
(35th Fighter Squadron)
15 Mar 44, 1 Zero
27 Jul 44, 1 Oscar
2 Nov 44, 3 Hamps
4 Nov 44, 3 Oscars
6 Nov 44, 1 Tony
15 Nov 44, 1 Oscar

Paul M. Stanch
(39th Fighter Squadron)
3 Mar 43, 2 Fighters
4 Mar 43, 1 Fighter
21 Jul 43, 2 Oscars
23 Jul 43, 1 Fighter

Murray J. Shubin
(339 Fighter Squadron)
2 Feb 43, 1 Zero
7 Jun 43, 1 Zero
16 Jun 43, 5 Zeros
10 Oct 43, 2 Zeros
27 Oct 43, 2 Val

2 Sep 43, 1 Twin-Engine
22 Sep 43, 2 Zeros
23 Oct 43, 1 Oscar

Elliot Summer
432nd Fighter Squadron
21 Aug 43, 1 Zero
15 Oct 43, 1 Oscar
24 Oct 43, 1 Oscar
21 Dec 43, 2 Vals
22 Dec 43, 1 Zero
3 Apr 44, 1 Oscar
12 Nov 44, 2 Zeros
7 Dec 44, 1 Zero

Walter R. Duke (10 AF)
(459th Fighter Squadron)
11 Mar 44, 2 Oscars
25 Mar 44, ½ Oscar
17 Apr 44, 1 Oscar
23 Apr 44, ½ Tojo
25 Apr 44, 1 Oscar
29 Apr 44, 1 Oscar
3 May 44, 1 Oscar
7 May 44, 1 Oscar
19 May 44, 1 Oscar
23 May 44, 1 Oscar
6 Jun 44, 3 Zeros

Michael Brezas
(48th Fighter Squadron)
8 Jul 44, 1 Me 109
14 Jul 44, 2 Me 210s; 1 Fw 190
19 Jul 44, 1 Fw 190
20 Jul 44, 1 Me 109
22 Jul 44, 2 Fw 190s
7 Aug 44, 2 Me 109s
25 Aug 44, 2 Fw 190s

William Leverette
(37th Fighter Squadron)
9 Oct 43, 7 Ju 87
14 Dec 43, 1 Me 109
24 Feb 44, 1 Me 110
18 Mar 44, 1 Me 109
12 Apr 44, 1 Me 110